THE BLACK ARTS
MOVEMENT

Creating a Cultural Identity

By Vanessa Oswald

Portions of this book originally appeared in
The Black Arts Movement by David Robson.

LUCENT
PRESS

Published in 2020 by
Lucent Press, an Imprint of Greenhaven Publishing, LLC
353 3rd Avenue
Suite 255
New York, NY 10010

Designer: Deanna Paternostro
Editor: Vanessa Oswald

Library of Congress Cataloging-in-Publication Data

Names: Oswald, Vanessa, author.
Title: The Black Arts movement : creating a cultural identity / Vanessa
  Oswald.
Description: [First edition]. | New York : Lucent Press, 2020. | Series:
  Lucent library of black history | Includes bibliographical references and
  index.
Identifiers: LCCN 2019018268 (print) | LCCN 2019018901 (ebook) | ISBN
  9781534568549 (eBook) | ISBN 9781534568532 (library bound book) | ISBN
  9781534568525 (pbk. book)
Subjects: LCSH: Black Arts movement. | Arts and society–United
  States–History–20th century.
Classification: LCC NX512.3.A35 (ebook) | LCC NX512.3.A35 O89 2020 (print) |
  DDC 700.89/96073–dc23
LC record available at https://lccn.loc.gov/2019018268

Printed in China

Some of the images in this book illustrate individuals who are models. The depictions do not imply
actual situations or events.

CPSIA compliance information: Batch #BW20KL: For further information contact Greenhaven Publishing LLC, New York, New York at 1-844-317-7404.

Please visit our website, www.greenhavenpublishing.com. For a free color catalog of all our
high-quality books, call toll free 1-844-317-7404 or fax 1-844-317-7405.

CONTENTS

FOREWORD

From medicine and law to sports and literature, African Americans have played a major role in the history of the United States. However, these groundbreaking men and women often faced prejudice and persecution. More than 300 years ago, Africans were taken in chains from their home and enslaved to work for the earliest American settlers. They suffered for more than two centuries under the brutal oppression of their owners until the outbreak of the American Civil War in 1861. After the dust settled four years later and thousands of Americans—both black and white—had died in combat, slavery in the United States had been legally abolished. By the turn of the 20th century, with the help of the 13th, 14th, and 15th Amendments to the U.S. Constitution, African American men had finally won significant battles for the basic rights of citizenship, but the fight for equality was far from over. Even after the successes of the civil rights movement, the struggle continued—and it still continues today.

Although the history of the African American experience is not always a pleasant story, it is also filled with powerful moments of positive change. These triumphs of human equality were achieved with help from brave social activists such as Frederick Douglass, Martin Luther King Jr., and Maya Angelou. They all experienced racial prejudice in their lifetimes and fought by writing, speaking, and acting against it. By exposing the suffering of the black community, they brought people together to try to remedy centuries' worth of wrongdoing.

Today, it is important to learn about the history of African Americans and their experiences in modern America in order to work toward healing the divide that still exists in the United States. This series aims to give readers a deeper appreciation for and understanding of a part of the American story that is often left untold.

Even before the legal emancipation of slaves, black culture was thriving despite many attempts to suppress it. From music to language to art, slaves began cultivating an identity that was completely unique. Soon after these slaves were granted citizenship, African American culture burst into the mainstream. New generations of authors, scholars, painters, and singers were born, and they spread an appreciation for black culture across America and the entire world. Studying the contributions of these talented individuals fosters a sense of optimism. Despite the cruel treatment and racist attitudes these men and women faced, they never gave up, and they helped change the world with their determination and unique voices.

The Lucent Library of Black History offers a glimpse into the lives and accomplishments of some of the most important and influential African Americans across historical time periods and areas of interest. From the arts and sports to the military and politics, the wide variety of topics allows readers to get a full and clear picture of the successes and struggles African Americans have experienced and are continuing to experience. Titles examine primary source documents and quotes from historical and modern figures to provide an enriching learning experience for readers. With detailed timelines, unique sidebars, and a carefully selected bibliography for further research, this series gives readers the tools to independently discover historical events and figures that do not often get their time in the spotlight.

By balancing the harsh realities of the past and present with a sense of hopefulness for the future, the Lucent Library of Black History helps young people understand an essential truth: Black history is a vital part of American history.

SETTING THE SCENE:

April 13, 1964
Sidney Poitier wins the Academy Award for Best Actor for the 1963 film *Lilies of the Field*; making him the first African American to win in this category.

February 21, 1965
Malcolm X is assassinated at the Audubon Ballroom in Harlem in New York City. He was shot by three gunman who were members of the Nation of Islam.

1964   1965   1966

1965
The Black Arts Repertory Theatre and School (BARTS), founded by LeRoi Jones, opens in Harlem at the start of the Black Arts movement.

August 11, 1965
Race riots begin in Los Angeles after Marquette Frye, an African American driver, is pulled over and arrested by Lee W. Minikus, a white police officer, who suspected him of drunk driving.

1964
James Chaney, a black civil rights leader, and Jewish men Andrew Goodman and Michael "Mickey" Schwerner are killed near Philadelphia, Mississippi, by Klansmen in police uniforms.

October 15, 1966
The Black Panther Party is founded by Bobby Seale and Huey Newton.

6

A TIMELINE

1967
The New Lafayette Theatre,
founded by Robert Macbeth,
opens in Harlem.

April 4, 1968
Martin Luther King Jr. is assassinated at
the Lorraine Motel in Memphis, Tennessee.
He is pronounced dead at St. Joseph's
Hospital in Memphis. James Earl Ray
pleaded guilty to King's murder, but he
later said he was the victim of a conspiracy.

1967   1968   1975

1975
The Black Arts
movement ends.

1968
Nathan Hare joins San Francisco
State College and becomes the
program coordinator of the
school's black studies program,
the first in the United States.

INTRODUCTION

EARLY HISTORY OF BLACK ART

The roots leading to the creation of the Black Arts movement extend as far back as before the issuing of the Emancipation Proclamation on January 1, 1863. Slaves used their art for practical purposes and to expose the horrible conditions they were subjected to. Slave songs, or spirituals, handmade quilts, and poetry did more than express a link to slaves' African past; folklore states that they may have contained coded messages encouraging slaves to quietly escape from bondage. Some stories tell of popular quilting patterns that were sometimes used as guideposts for escapees or were hung outside a slave's quarters as a signal to others looking to run away.

Before and during the American Civil War, abolitionists published slave poems in their newspapers as a way of gaining members. The poems themselves often reported the dreadful conditions of slaves, including long hours in the hot sun and daily whippings. Despite the practical and secretive nature of slave art, care had to be taken. Owners generally viewed communication between slaves as a danger to their valuable property. They also frowned on teaching slaves to read. After all, as writer and orator Frederick Douglass suggested, an educated slave would be less likely to want to remain a slave. Eventually, this could lead to more slaves participating in resistance and revolts against their masters.

Activists of the Black Arts movement, and others before its prominence who paved the way, worked tirelessly to create a world where a black person's voice could be heard and taken seriously among white people. One crucial activist who voiced his opinions on the treatment and future of black people was a man by the name of Malcolm Little, known to most as Malcolm X.

Starting a Cultural Revolution

The day Malcolm X died marked the birth of the Black Arts movement. On Sunday, February 21, 1965, the former convict and controversial civil rights icon Malcolm X was scheduled to speak at New York City's Audubon Ballroom. Only a week before, Malcolm X's family home had been firebombed; his pregnant wife, Betty, and four young children barely escaped with their lives. For two years, Malcolm X had told the media that his life was in grave danger, yet the outspoken leader refused to back down.

Whether speaking out against white racism or, more recently, the corruption of his former organization, the Nation of Islam, Malcolm X tempted fate daily. His willingness to consider violence and separation from white America in the struggle for racial justice contrasted sharply with the philosophy of the Reverend Dr. Martin Luther King Jr. King, the brilliant and outspoken leader of the civil rights movement, preached a message of nonviolence and integration. However, like many in the African American community, Malcolm X believed King and his movement were too willing to compromise on important issues with a white establishment that black Americans viewed as racist.

While in jail years before, Malcolm X had discovered Islam and started reading several books on the tortured history of African Americans. "I will never forget how shocked I was when I began reading about slavery's total horror," he wrote in his autobiography. "The world's most monstrous crime, the sin and blood on the white man's hands, are almost impossible to believe."[1]

It was, he said, essential for black people to reconnect with their proud past, a past rooted in the traditions of their African heritage that had been stolen from them. Thus, a year before his death, standing before an audience in Harlem, Malcolm X encouraged black Americans to rediscover

Malcolm X was one of the most influential figures in black history.

themselves: "We must recapture our heritage and our identity if we are ever to liberate ourselves from the bonds of white supremacy. We must launch a cultural revolution to *unbrainwash* an entire people."[2]

Over the next decade, an underground movement of writers, painters, poets, and musicians would rise to take the fallen leader's words to heart. The Black Arts movement would one day sprout in almost every corner of the United States, with its new leaders encouraging political action and a return to the past for inspiration.

In time, both whites and blacks would criticize the movement for its refusal to stand down when it came to polarizing politics and for its exclusion of white culture and influence. Then, just as the Black Arts movement began taking hold, it vanished.

Defining the Black Arts Movement

The Black Arts movement served as the artistic branch of the Black Power movement, which attempted to create the cultural revolution Malcolm X spoke of. Black Power, a strain of black nationalism, evolved on a parallel track with the American civil rights movement. However, black nationalist ideas and tactics were considered more radical and less peaceful than those of the civil rights movement, which stressed nonviolence. If King was the spokesperson for mainstream civil rights, then the equally eloquent Malcolm X spoke for black nationalists.

Although black artists and publications began thriving years earlier, the clock for the Black Arts movement began running the day of Malcolm X's assassination. Those artists and thinkers sympathetic to Malcolm X's ideas were outraged, though perhaps not surprised, by his murder. Collectively, they were determined to carry on his ideas of separatism and revolution.

The Black Arts movement was large and complex, but it was also somewhat discrete, as members carried no identification cards and there were no monthly meetings. However, African American artists of the time were inspired by a sense of growing cultural identity. In that sense, it was a movement that moved people. Musicians, sculptors, poets, painters, novelists, and playwrights led the charge. While they worked sometimes thousands of miles apart, in groups or alone, what unified them was a desire to change American life forever—and to do it on their own terms.

The Importance of the Black Arts Movement

The Black Arts movement was a cultural

landmark in American history that paved the way for diversity in American arts and popular culture and broadened acceptance of minority voices in the visual, literary, and performing arts. It also recognized that "African Americans had a common history and a distinct national culture,"[3] said scholar James Edward Smethurst.

This recognition was essential because black culture was typically deemed inferior to that of whites. The Black Arts movement began transforming this view from the inside out. It encouraged self-reliance, political engagement, and a break from a white culture that continually rejected it. "Its function," wrote critic Henry Louis Gates Jr., "was to serve the political liberation of black people from white racism."[4]

Although the movement lasted only a decade and ended in 1975, it helped transform the notion of what it means to be an African American. Its words, music, and images cast a shadow that is still visible in the 21st century.

Influence on American Culture Today

Although the Black Arts movement was short-lived, its influence on black artists was not. Art created by African Americans is more popular today than ever before. The cultural avalanche of black art, so long in coming, is still being felt across the United States.

From the prize-winning jazz compositions of Wynton Marsalis to the thought-provoking films of Spike Lee; from the lyrical prose of Edward P. Jones to the politically conscious rap of Kendrick Lamar—the revolution is televised around the world every day and blasted from millions of car speakers. "It's not that there are black artists and intellectuals who matter," Gates said. "It's that so many artists and intellectuals who matter are black."[5] The difference, he suggested, is one of influence and acceptance—not despite racial differences but because of them.

These artists continue to produce art, sharing a range of meaningful ideas with the world about black history, Black Power, black struggle, and the future of black people as a whole. For years, their art has expressed the truth, joy, strife, and angst of a group that has been discriminated against for centuries. However, art gave them an outlet through which to filter their unique and passionate voices to help the rest of society imagine life from their perspectives.

CHAPTER ONE

THE ORIGINS OF
BLACK NATIONALISM

The history surrounding Africans before they were sold into slavery through the transatlantic slave trade was previously unknown and blurred over the years. Only in the last 50 years has the history of the African people been rediscovered. It is now known that their civilizations were some of the first to have unearthed scientific developments. They also created some of the first states and monarchies.

Long after white colonists enslaved Africans in the Americas, black nationalism was born. It is the idea that black people share a common identity and destiny. It hinges on the principles of racial pride and independence from white society. The painful history of slavery and the subsequent political and social oppression of African Americans in North America is crucial in understanding black nationalism and, subsequently, the Black Arts movement.

In their brutal journey from small villages in western Africa to the shores of the American colonies—later known as the United States—enslaved black people lost more than their freedom. They also lost their native cultures. Forced to abide by the rules of their captors, African Americans were stripped of their past and, consequently, their identity. It would take hundreds of years and the vision of great artists, thinkers, and revolutionaries to begin restoring ownership of these identities.

A Horrific Experience

During the height of the transatlantic slave trade, from the 1500s through the 1800s, roughly 15 million Africans were sold into slavery around the world. Today the American descendants of slaves number 40 million. The story of the slave trade is one of suffering and death.

The journey into slavery could take months, as war prisoners, refugees, and other unlucky individuals in countries such as Sierra Leone and Ghana were captured and bound at the neck with rope or chains. Next came the back-breaking "Long March"—perhaps as long as 300 miles (483 km)—from the interior of the country to the sea, where a cargo ship waited along the coast. Because slave ships often stopped at many ports to capture and shackle more slaves, the infamous Middle Passage could take up to 10 months.

The average slave ship held 350 Africans. Below deck, men were chained flat in pairs in spaces 16 inches (40.6 cm) wide and 5 feet (1.5 m) long. Women and children remained unchained and were allowed occasionally to roam the deck. The conditions were horrendous. Nigerian Olaudah Equiano, who went on to write the first known slave narrative in the late 1700s, spoke of the smells and sounds: "The stench of the hold ... became absolutely pestilential ... The shrieks of the women, and the groans of the dying,

Africans were put on ships that sailed across the Atlantic Ocean, and then sold into slavery by colonists during the time of the transatlantic slave trade.

rendered the whole a scene of horror."[6] Although Equiano survived his ordeal, he never forgot the experience.

Those slaves who arrived alive on the other side of the world staggered from the ship's hold sick and debilitated, only to be sold to owners who often mistreated them and separated them from their families. Although officially banned in 1808, the Atlantic slave trade did not truly end in the United States until 1860. After nearly 300 years, slaves remained deprived of their native languages and customs.

The Emancipation Proclamation in 1863 and the end of the Civil War in 1865 did little to improve the everyday lives of African Americans. Between 1877 and the early 1970s, southern Jim Crow laws kept blacks and whites separated. Some of these laws were enforced by local, state, and federal governments; others simply existed out of custom. Charles George wrote: "Since blacks were never considered equal to whites, they were expected to call all whites 'master' and 'mistress,' speak only when spoken to, and never look a white person directly in the eye. Thus, a tradition of control of one race by another was established."[7]

Marcus Garvey's Mission

As the 20th century dawned, African American leaders such as Booker T. Washington and W.E.B. Du Bois charted a course toward reconciliation with whites. Principally, the call was for integration; blacks and whites would be treated equally in all facets of American life. However, this proved unrealistic to many Americans.

For its part, much of black America craved leadership it could relate to and understand. The time was right for a national movement—one that promoted racial pride and change. The time was right for outspoken leadership of the kind that Marcus Garvey specialized in. He was a supporter of Pan-Africanism, which is similar to black nationalism; it is a global movement encouraging the solidarity between all people of African descent, focusing on specific aspects, such as politics, ideology, organizations, and culture.

While growing up in St. Ann's Bay, Jamaica, Garvey rarely saw the ugly side of racism. His family was far from rich, but they never went hungry. Garvey's father worked as a mason, while his mother raised crops to sell and for the family's dinner table. One of his best friends, Joyce Rerrie, was a white girl; neither child ever questioned the color of each other's skin. They only knew that they enjoyed playing games and spending time with one another.

When Marcus and Joyce became

teenagers, everything changed. Joyce was sent to England at the age of 14; her father warned her to stay away from Marcus because he was black. For the first time in his young life, Marcus was forced to confront his race. "He felt shut out," Robert Hill wrote. "He felt that he was excluded and made to feel that he was not good enough, and the rest of his life was really an attempt to prove that he was just as good as anyone else in the world."[8] As he grew to adulthood, Marcus Garvey developed his reading, writing, and speaking skills. He dreamed of becoming a great leader, but he knew he had to venture beyond St. Ann's Bay to achieve this dream.

In 1910, Garvey traveled to Central America, working as a journalist and day laborer along the way. During his travels he witnessed firsthand the bloody legacy of colonialism. For most native peoples, their countries were not their own; instead, European powers controlled the natural resources and, thus, the wealth. Far from Jamaica, Garvey saw men and women, dark-skinned like him, working for little money on plantations, loading ships, and constructing the Panama Canal. As he realized these people were powerless, he decided this had to change.

As he matured, Garvey began to see himself as a leader of the people. When he returned to Jamaica, after being inspired by the book *Up from Slavery* by Washington, he founded the Universal Negro Improvement Association

Marcus Garvey founded the Universal Negro Improvement Association.

(UNIA) in 1914. The goal of the organization was to uplift black people by giving them something—and someone—to believe in. In Garvey's words, the UNIA's purpose was in "uniting all the negro peoples of the world into one great body to establish a country and Government absolutely their own."[9]

Yet in Garvey's homeland, the UNIA quickly failed. Despite his personal charisma and passion, Garvey also had a talent for making enemies. He attacked local leaders, was intolerant of other ideas, and misused UNIA contributions reserved for a school. Soon after, he left Jamaica again, this time under less pleasant circumstances.

Garvey's New Recruits

Despite his mistakes, Garvey marched on, arriving in New York City penniless yet determined to remake himself and spread his nationalistic vision in 1916. For a time he lived with a Jamaican family, working in a print shop by day, speaking to those who would listen by night. He started on street corners and before long was drawing substantial crowds. Urban black communities yearned for strong and revolutionary leadership, and soon Garvey's ideas of racial pride and self-determination caught on. "Be as proud of your race today as our fathers were in the days of yore," Garvey said. "We have a beautiful history. And we shall create another in the future that will astonish the world."[10] With words like these, considered radical in their time, Garvey's UNIA would capture the imaginations of black people in 38 states and 41 countries around the world.

Several black leaders in the 1920s were preaching integration as a way of bridging the gap of inequality between the races. However, Garvey disagreed with this tactic. He refused to support the assimilation policies of contemporaries like sociologist Du Bois and union organizer A. Philip Randolph. Randolph, editor of the influential *Messenger* magazine, had arranged Garvey's first formal speaking engagement. Yet as the UNIA grew in popularity, Garvey rejected Randolph and other integrationists, labeling them weak. Many of his followers agreed.

Garvey challenged black people to band together and fight back against oppression and the despicable Jim Crow laws of the South. Never before had a black leader so boldly called for people of color to stand up for themselves and take what was rightfully theirs. Even more shocking was Garvey's ambitious goal of creating an independent black nation, possibly in an African country—an original goal of Pan-Africanism. This

GARVEY'S WIVES

Marcus Garvey was not the only black empowerment activist helping to start organizations that made black people feel like their voices were being heard. During his lifetime, he was married twice, and both of his wives participated in these endeavors of bringing transparency to the black person's struggle.

In 1914, he returned to Kingston, Jamaica, to attend a debate, and he witnessed a powerful political speech delivered by Pan-Africanist and feminist Amy Ashwood. He was moved by her words and approached her on the trolley as they were heading home. This same year, they launched the Universal Negro Improvement Association (UNIA). In 1918, she organized a women's section of the UNIA and together they founded the *Negro World* weekly newspaper. While serving as Garvey's aide, she was made the secretary of the UNIA's New York City branch. Garvey later made her secretary of the Black Star Line (a shipping line created to transport goods and eventually African Americans) in 1919, which was also the year they were married. However, the couple divorced shortly after in 1922, and Garvey quickly married Ashwood's former roommate Amy Jacques, who was also from Kingston.

Jacques was also an activist, specifically for Pan-African emancipation, and a journalist. She moved to Harlem, New York, where she met Garvey in 1917. As a journalist, she became involved with the *Negro World* newspaper and produced a section titled "Our Women and What They Think," addressing feminist issues. She also took on editing the three volumes of *The Philosophy and Opinions of Marcus Garvey*, a compilation of Garvey's writings and speeches. These texts were created for people to read so they could make up their own minds about Garvey, instead of believing many biased sources of the time.

would require blacks' complete economic and social separation from white America and a return to the roots and traditions once stripped from them. Most African Americans knew little about Africa, and what they did get—from newspapers and movies—was misleading. Garvey supporter Charles Mills explained: "Africa was called the 'Dark Continent,' and the pictures we got of Africa in those days were cannibals running around in the jungles, puttin' people in pots. Garvey changed all that."[11]

Most importantly, the UNIA was a movement of the masses, not an exclusionary club for intellectuals. It encouraged broad membership; any black person could join. The requirements included a fee of 35 cents, a photograph, and a signed pledge of support. In return, African Americans from all walks of life were given something to believe in. They listened to their outspoken leader on the radio; read his newspaper, the *Negro World*; and marched with him in parades through Harlem or down Fifth Avenue, waving the red, black, and green flag of their nation in the making.

Garvey carried his groundbreaking message of change all across the country. It was a message that would one day serve as inspiration for the Black Arts movement. However, in the early 1920s, white America could only watch in astonishment. "I am the equal of any white man," said Garvey. "I want you [other blacks] to feel the same way."[12] Such rhetoric frightened white Americans, most of whom viewed the social order—with whites in control—as permanent.

At the height of his popularity, Garvey received many death threats from whites and harsh criticism from integrationist blacks. In 1922, one group, A. Philip Randolph's Friends of Negro Freedom, worked to undermine Garvey's hold on African Americans. However, in the end, it was accusations of more financial wrongdoing that led to Garvey's and the UNIA's downfall. Despite the movement's ultimate failure, several influential activist nationalist groups emerged after being influenced by the Garvey movement. In time, Garvey's work became a touchstone for the artists and organizers who followed.

Emergence of the Harlem Renaissance

Just as Marcus Garvey was pitching his message of black nationalism, young Missouri-born Langston Hughes was finding his poetic voice. Traveling by train to visit his father in Mexico, Hughes one day gazed out the window at the desert scenery rolling by and put pen to paper. He wrote of deep rivers, old rivers and connected them to the African American experience.

Hughes's signature poem became "The Negro Speaks of Rivers," which was published for the first time in 1921 in the magazine *The Crisis*. Although he was only 19 when he wrote the poem, Hughes's distinctive, confident voice would soon help power the 20th century's first major African American artistic movement.

In his poem, Hughes blends a contemporary voice with the outlines of a rich and ancient African history—a history that predates slavery. For so long, this unique and dignified collective past went unacknowledged or was forgotten by most Americans, black or white.

In time, Hughes came to be known as the father of the Harlem Renaissance, an explosion of black artistic expression in the 1920s and 1930s. However, Hughes only capitalized on a movement that was already paved by others.

Just after World War I, scholar James Weldon Johnson, encouraged by journalist H.L. Mencken, began calling for change for black people. Johnson recognized that black people had fought and died for the country, most recently in World War I, but they were still given little respect. Despite Marcus Garvey's best efforts and his millions of followers, African Americans remained second-class citizens. For Johnson, racial inequality and injustice was a matter of mindset. His solution was profound and revolutionary. "Nothing will do more to change this mental attitude and raise [the black man's] status," he wrote, "than ... through the production of literature and art."[13] There were not enough positive images of black people, Johnson believed, and only through

Langston Hughes's poetry was referenced by many who supported the Black Arts movement.

self-expression could such images be created.

The New Negro movement, as the Harlem Renaissance was then known, also embraced Africa itself. "Through much of the writing ran a spirit of optimism ... that celebrated African Americans' survival of a harsh past in the United States, their legacy of a rich cultural past on the African continent, and their expectation of better days ahead,"[14] historian Robert J. Norrell said.

Despite the call for optimism and

a look homeward, in the summer of 1919, race riots broke out in a number of American cities. The riots were sparked primarily by high unemployment and a lack of opportunities for those men returning from the war. Returning whites were angered because they now had to compete with blacks for jobs. During this "Red Summer," as it came to be known, whites attacked blacks in northern and southern cities alike, including Omaha, Nebraska; Washington, D.C.; Longview, Texas; and Chicago, Illinois.

Jamaican-born Claude McKay, like much of the country, read about the violent riots in the newspaper. He poured his emotions into a poem titled "If We Must Die," which was published in 1919. He acknowledged that the death of black people might be inevitable. However, he wrote, the deaths would not be in vain if people died nobly and with convictions. The sonnet, or a poem composed of fourteen lines, also called the white murderers "monsters" and his poem ends with a call to self-defense.

McKay's black man was no weak, pathetic creature; he was strong enough to defend himself against the violence and the racism that had, for so long, troubled his people. His poem was widely read as a call to arms, and 45 years later, black artists heeded this call and took their struggle far beyond what McKay could have dreamed.

While McKay's poem may have pushed open the door to black expression, it was the 1925 publication of the anthology *The New Negro: An Interpretation*, edited by Alain Locke,

In response to the 1919 race riots, Claude McKay wrote the poem "If We Must Die."

that kicked the door in once and for all. Before long—and with the aid of white artists and patrons of the arts—black writers were being published in established, previously white-dominated magazines such as the *Nation* and *Vanity Fair* and winning book contracts with major publishing firms.

One white supporter of the budding movement was Carl Van Vechten, a photographer and music critic who used his influence in New York City to bring together African American writers and powerful publishers. His 1926 novel *N***** Heaven*, an enticing portrait of the Harlem nightlife, was labeled exploitation by some critics, including Du Bois. Yet through his efforts and connections, Van Vechten was able to increase the nation's demand for the work of African Americans like Hughes, McKay, Jean Toomer, Countee Cullen, and Zora Neale Hurston.

As for the artists themselves, they were determined to chart a new artistic course, one that rejected the history of European-influenced expression. It was, they insisted, time to stop imitating their former masters' works and begin celebrating the dignity and creativity brought to America's shores hundreds of years before.

In his famous essay "The Negro Artist and the Racial Mountain," Hughes brushed aside the notion, held by many white Americans since the days of slavery, that the lives of African Americans were unworthy of art. He spoke for and to black artists of all types, as well as whites who might be suspicious of the power and influence of African American creativity:

> *There is sufficient material to furnish a black artist with a lifetime of creative work. And when he chooses to touch on the relations between Negroes and whites … there is an inexhaustible supply of themes at hand. To these the Negro artist can give his racial individuality, his heritage of rhythm and warmth, and his incongruous humor that so often, as in the Blues, becomes ironic laughter mixed with tears. But let us look again at the mountain.*[15]

The mountain, as Hughes saw it, was "this urge within the [black] race toward whiteness."[16] However, instead of looking to whites, he suggested that black artists must look within. Hughes's essay became a rallying cry, a gauntlet thrown down not in anger, but in confidence and certainty.

In the years to come, many in the Black Arts movement would sneer at the perceived foolishness of the Harlem Renaissance, a movement

A FEMALE WRITER ALMOST FORGOTTEN

Perhaps the most significant female writer of the Harlem Renaissance was Eatonville, Florida, native Zora Neale Hurston. Born in Alabama but steeped in the dialect and traditions of Eatonville, Hurston studied anthropology at Barnard College with famed anthropologist Franz Boas. Her first book, *Mules and Men* (1935), is a collection of African American folklore and mythology. As her studies continued, Hurston became involved with the fledgling literary movement in Harlem. There she met Hughes and other notable writers. Later, Hurston traveled throughout the Caribbean collecting stories and studying the native peoples. Her best-known work, *Their Eyes Were Watching God* (1937), tells the story of mixed-race Janie Crawford. Janie is a tough and independent woman who suffers physical and emotional hardships before meeting Tea Cake, a younger man with whom she finds happiness before tragedy strikes.

By the 1950s, Hurston's work had been virtually forgotten. Although Hurston continued to write, she never again got to see her work in wide circulation. Then, in the summer of 1973, writer Alice Walker, who would write the 1982 novel *The Color Purple*, searched for Hurston's grave, discovering it in an overgrown and forgotten segregated cemetery in Fort Pierce, Florida. In 1979, when Walker wrote her first essay on Hurston, all of Hurston's books were out of print. "Her work had a sense of black people as complete, complex, undiminished human beings and that was crucial to me as a writer," Walker said. "I loved the way Zora showed the light and the beauty and spirit of black people. She loved her own culture, especially the language."[1] Today, Hurston is widely read and respected.

Zora Neale Hurston was one of the most influential female writers during the Harlem Renaissance.

1. Quoted in "Alice Walker Shines Light on Zora Neale Hurston," PBS, accessed on January 24, 2019. www.pbs.org/wnet/americanmasters/alice-walker-film-excerpt-walker-puts-zora-neale-hurston-back-in-spotlight/2869/.

financially supported in large part by white patrons like Van Vechten. Hughes and his contemporaries had not gone far enough in building a separate, distinct artistic vision, the critics would complain. Still, the Harlem Renaissance gave voice to the challenges facing African Americans and paved the way for the next steps along the road of social acceptance and change.

Civil Rights Progression

Despite the positive steps taken during the Harlem Renaissance, better days for African Americans were still a long way off. In his searing 1952 novel *Invisible Man*, Ralph Ellison, a novelist deeply influenced by the Harlem Renaissance, spoke for so many African Americans in the famous opening lines: "I am an invisible man. No, I am not a spook like those who haunted Edgar Allan Poe; nor am I one of your Hollywood-movie ectoplasms. I am a man of substance, of flesh and bone, fiber and liquids—and I might even be said to possess a mind. I am invisible, understand, simply because people refuse to see me."[17]

When not invisible, black people suffered blatant racism. Despite the awareness and respect given to the black experience in the years following the Harlem Renaissance, the nation's laws remained discriminatory and racist. However, a legal transformation on the horizon would bring hope to black people.

As empowered activists fought for the rights of black people during the civil rights movement, a 1954 Supreme Court decision broke with southern tradition and sent shock waves through the United States. *Brown v. Board of Education of Topeka* made the integration of public schools mandatory across the country. Until then, the law had required a "separate but equal" policy that in reality left most black schoolchildren with rundown schools and outdated textbooks.

In 1955, civil rights activist Rosa Parks refused to move to the back of the bus, a requirement for all southern African Americans at the time. Parks's calculated civil disobedience sparked the Montgomery, Alabama, bus boycott. The boycott lasted 381 days—more than a year—until the city's financially strapped bus company gave in, which finally allowed black people to sit anywhere they liked.

The boycott was led by a brash and outspoken young minister named Martin Luther King Jr. King's tactics of nonviolence, borrowed from Indian leader Mohandas Gandhi, struck a chord with white and black America. His triumphant speeches and writings inspired millions to follow his dream of integration, equality, and peace.

The seeds of black nationalism and

Martin Luther King Jr. fought for the civil rights of black people. However, he stressed to them that the way to do it was through nonviolence.

radical rethinking of the tactics used in fighting a system built by and for white Americans: They would not ask for change, they would demand it; they would no longer rely on whites for support and instead would support each other; and no longer could blacks reject violence, as King did. Too many of them had died at the hands of whites.

Often considered the antithesis, or opposite, of King, black nationalist leader Malcolm X made it plain: "Our enemy is the white man." Like Marcus Garvey 40 years earlier, Malcolm X called for a separate nation, "a land of our own, where we can reform ourselves, lift up our moral standards, and try to be godly."[18]

the Black Arts movement sprouted at the same time as the civil rights movement. However, it rejected the idea of integration and assimilation with white America. For black nationalists, King, despite his good intentions, was not the answer to their problems. He and his movement were too eager to negotiate with whites, they believed; negotiation was a sign of weakness, not strength. Black nationalists also called for a

The Black Arts movement aimed for such reform through words, music, visual arts, and action, but it would do so without its leader. However, his influence would shine through the art made to showcase black empowerment. Black artists were inspired to create like never before with confidence and vigor to promote the history of their ancestors that had been unobserved for so long by a society run by the white man.

CHAPTER TWO
THE EMERGENCE OF THE BLACK ARTS MOVEMENT

On the night of February 21, 1965, there came a turning point in the lives of many black people in the United States. Malcolm X was dead. He was gunned down in cold blood in front of hundreds of people at the Audubon Ballroom in Harlem. LeRoi Jones, a renowned 31-year-old poet and playwright, read the tragic news in the evening paper that night. Reading the accounts of the assassination over and over again, he was shattered to hear the story of how his hero had died.

For this particular event, 400 wooden chairs had been set up. When Malcolm X's young assistant arrived at 1:30 p.m., she noticed at least four men had already taken their seats directly in front of the stage. She thought nothing of it; it was common for audience members to come early. Malcolm X was world famous, not only for his views on black nationalism but for the fiery nature of his speeches. The thin, impassioned leader had the unique ability to captivate onlookers with his well-crafted words, his vocal power, and his dark, steely eyes.

Nearly half an hour later, the ballroom was nearly full. Despite the dangers, Malcolm X had rejected the idea of searching people at the door for weapons. "It makes people uncomfortable," he said. "If I can't be safe among my own kind, where can I be?"[19]

At almost 2:00 p.m., Malcolm X arrived and took a seat backstage. The man who was to introduce him, Reverend Galamison, was late. In his place, Malcolm X sent his aide Benjamin X to speak to the excited crowd. By 3:00 p.m., Galamison still had not shown, and Benjamin X introduced his mentor. Striding to the podium, Malcolm X looked confident. He offered the crowd the familiar Muslim

Malcolm X was speaking to a crowd of over 400 people at the Audubon Ballroom in Harlem the day he was shot.

Jones Kick-Starts the Movement

To Jones, the bullets that punctured Malcolm X were the shots heard around the black world. Continued racial injustice and the murder of his idol convinced Jones that the time was right for a radical rethinking of the role of black people in American society. In fact, he had already begun making his mark, not only as an activist for black nationalism, but also as a poet and playwright.

greeting: "*Asalaikum*, brothers and sisters!" Some in the audience responded, "Asalaikum salaam!"[20]

Suddenly, a scuffle broke out in the crowd—people pushing and shoving; Malcolm X tried to calm them. "Let's cool it, brothers,"[21] he said. However, the commotion distracted the speaker and audience long enough for at least three gunmen to approach the stage and begin firing. As the gunshots were fired, men, women, and children ran for cover. "I saw Malcolm hit with his hands still raised, then he fell back over the chairs behind him,"[22] radio station WMCA reporter Hugh Simpson said.

In 1964, Jones, who later became known as Amiri Baraka, electrified the New York theater world with his provocative one-act play, *Dutchman*. The play, set in a dingy New York City subway car, centered on a mild-mannered black man who is propositioned, abused, and then brutally stabbed by a white woman. Now, a year after the play's premiere, Jones was distraught and confused by the news of the day. In his autobiography, he echoed the feeling of helplessness so many black people felt: "Malcolm's death had thrown people up in the air like coins in a huge hairy hand."[23]

The Newark, New Jersey–born activist spent his artistically formative years in Greenwich Village in downtown Manhattan. There, Jones had lived an integrated life. Long connected with the American beat movement led by Jack Kerouac, many of his friends and even his wife, Hettie, were white. However, Jones, by the mid-1960s, could no longer relate to his white friends. He was seething with anger. During a speech at the Village Gate, a white woman stood up and asked Jones if whites could help blacks in some way. "You can help by dying," he told her. "You are a cancer. You can help the world's people with your death."[24] Jones said this out of anger to the white woman because of the killings on June 21, 1964, of James Chaney, a black man, and Andrew Goodman and Michael "Mickey" Schwerner, two Jewish men, in Philadelphia, Mississippi, by Klansmen in police uniforms. The three men had been working with the Freedom Summer campaign to register African Americans in Mississippi to vote. However, the majority of people responding to this horrific incident were only mentioning the deaths of Goodman and Schwerner and failing to mention the death of Chaney, which infuriated Jones, leading him to lash out at white people, even when they were asking what they could do to help.

The day after Malcolm X's assassination, Jones held a press conference in New York, announcing his plans to open the Black Arts Repertory Theatre and School (BARTS). A month later, Jones arrived in Harlem, moving into a brownstone on 130th Street. Harlem had been the center of African

LeRoi Jones was deeply moved by Malcolm X's death. He wanted to influence people's perceptions of blacks in American society through poetry, playwriting, and activism.

American culture for generations and this relocation marked a new beginning for the black artistic movement. His goal was to "help raise the race,"[25] and bring black culture to the forefront of society. It was, for Jones, a return to the roots of African American art and experience—a continuation of where it all began.

The new theater and school attracted African Americans from all over the East Coast. The theater held classes in poetry, playwriting, music, and painting. As a sign of the Black Arts movement's growing influence—and perceived threat to white America—two FBI agents decided to take a history course taught by Harold Cruse, author of *The Crisis of the Negro Intellectual*. The agents apparently sought to better understand the growing movement and its potential danger to the white establishment.

Jones had help from writer and friend Larry Neal in forging his unique vision for the future of black culture. Neal, who was born in Atlanta, Georgia, had moved north and earned his degrees at Lincoln University in Pennsylvania in the early 1960s. Later, Neal's writing on the importance of black art, in theater and elsewhere, became the touchstone for the Black Arts movement. In 1968, Neal, along with Jones, published *Black Fire*, an anthology of progressive black voices, including Cruse, Sonia Sanchez, Kwame Ture, and Stanley Crouch. The book came to be seen as the philosophical foundation for the movement and propelled Neal into the role of resident theorist. He called, among other things, for the weeding out of white and European influences in the art of African Americans. This artistic separatism was, Neal insisted, the only sure way to create a pure black aesthetic. Neal told *Ebony* magazine that the Black Arts movement "seeks to link ... art and politics in order to assist in the liberation of black people."[26]

Aside from community education, every Sunday, Jones, Neal, and other artists organized free concerts, poetry readings, and art shows. "We brought new music out in the streets ... vacant lots, playgrounds, parks," Jones wrote. "We had trucks with stages we designed from banquet tables, held together by clamps ... And Pharoah, Albert, Sun Ra, Trane, Cecil Taylor, and many other of the newest of the new came up and blew."[27]

Despite its initial success, the theater and school soon ran into financial trouble. Much of the organization's funding came from a Harlem antipoverty agency with ties to the state and federal government. However, its Afrocentric events and nationalistic goals made some white officials nervous, and the money dried up. This, along with internal struggles between its leaders, forced BARTS out of business, with it lasting less than a year. However, the experiment was not dead, and, in fact, was just beginning. In the wake of defeat, Jones moved back to his hometown of Newark, helped found an arts organization named Spirit House, continued writing, and changed his name to Amiri Baraka. He would be heard from again.

Integration of Black Theater

In New York, the Black Arts Repertory Theatre was only one part of a growing, citywide explosion of black performances. The New Lafayette Theatre in Harlem, founded in 1967, staged the works of many up-and-coming playwrights, also providing work for African American actors, stage managers, lighting designers, and costumers.

Started by Robert Macbeth, the New Lafayette hired playwright Ed Bullins as its writer-in-residence. Hailing from the San Francisco Bay Area, Bullins's popularity began to increase nationally. His plays, including *We Righteous Bombers* and *Goin' a Buffalo* were confrontational and stark, painting a bleak portrait of the bigotry and economic inequity inherent in the United States. *Goin' a Buffalo* centers on a group of

African Americans from Los Angeles who move to Buffalo, New York, seeking a better life to escape their lives of crime, only to find their dreams ruined. Bullins's bold work influenced the next generation of black playwrights, including Pulitzer Prize–winner August Wilson.

The New Lafayette, in time, was forced to move downtown after the theater was set on fire in 1968. Still, according to historian James Edward Smethurst, it became "a lightning rod for many of the intense debates"[28] over the direction of black art in New York City.

The National Black Theatre lasted longer and, like the New Lafayette, played an integral part in the growing influence of black performing arts. However, founder Barbara Ann Teer looked beyond the world of theater by encouraging members to broaden their experience with African American customs by attending black churches and other traditionally African American cultural activities.

Another long-standing organization with ties to the Black Arts movement is the New Federal Theatre. Led by director and writer Woodie King Jr., the New Federal still exists today. It has a reputation of presenting work by well-respected writers of color, including Charles Fuller, author of the award-winning *A Soldier's Play*, about murder and racism on a southern military base.

King's vision extended to other cultures as well. His original idea was that the New Federal would provide a venue for not only black theater but also for Asian, Jewish, and Latinx presentations as well. Still, despite the inclusive nature of the New Federal, King

BLACK PUBLISHERS

Initially, New York City was the black arts hub, but in other parts of the country too—small towns and big cities—black artists such as Sonia Sanchez and Nikki Giovanni were now finding their voices. At the same time, more outlets for black work were springing up, enabling these voices to reach the wider community.

Small publishers like Detroit's Broadside Press, founded by Dudley Randall in 1965, presented new poets in its pages, including Sanchez. Broadside is the oldest black-owned publishing press in the United States. Its first book project, a 1969 tribute anthology called *For Malcolm: Poems on the Life and the Death of Malcolm X*, exemplified Randall's mission: publishing inexpensive books that would appeal to a wide array of African American readers.

One contributor to *For Malcolm*, Haki R. Madhubuti, would soon become one of the best-selling poets in the country, with such volumes as *Black Pride* and *Don't Cry, Scream*. Madhubuti's commitment to the black community is reflected in his creation of another publishing house. Third World Press, housed in Chicago and started by Madhubuti, Carolyn Rodgers, and Jewel C. Latimore, dedicated itself to publishing works by Black Power activists. Their mission was to "provide in-depth reflections of ourselves by ourselves."[1]

Madhubuti, born Don L. Lee in the Deep South, had a difficult upbringing. His mother was a sex worker, and his sister gave birth to her first child at the age of 14. There were few places to turn for a young African American. Madhubuti said he grew up hating himself and felt confused and alone. However, he sought comfort in books; Richard Wright's *Black Boy* had a profound impact on him. Madhubuti later said that art saved his life. For Madhubuti, art also brought a deeper awareness of his culture and history, which eventually convinced him to change his birth name.

During the days of slavery, masters forced Anglo-Saxon or biblical first names and their family surnames on their human property. During the time remained adamant that "black plays should be directed by African American directors, Jewish plays by Jewish directors, and so on,"[29] Smethurst wrote.

One black playwright who knew all too well the challenge of being black and female in America was Adrienne Kennedy. Born and raised in Pittsburgh, Pennsylvania, Kennedy took an interest in drama early on and

of the Black Arts movement, more people of color took on traditional African names. For example, Malcolm X started life as Malcolm Little in Omaha, Nebraska. Upon joining the Nation of Islam, he used "X" as a tribute to his illiterate, enslaved ancestors, most of whom scrawled the letter when signing documents. Malcolm X was also known by the Islamic name El-Hajj Malik El-Shabazz. What was important is that some African Americans now chose their own names after centuries of being labeled by others. This act was an integral part of their self-determination.

Madhubuti and Randall's book publishing, as well as many journals such as *Black Dialogue, Umbra, Black America, Liberator,* and *Soulbook* helped define the Black Arts movement, providing a forum for an ongoing artistic and intellectual dialogue about historical, cultural, and social issues related to the black experience.

1. Quoted in Julius E. Thompson, *Dudley Randall, Broadside Press, and the Black Arts Movement in Detroit, 1960–1995.* Jefferson, NC: McFarland, 2005, p. 149.

Haki R. Madhubuti, who was committed to publishing works by Black Power activists, started Third World Press.

soon moved east, to New York City. There, she studied with Pulitzer Prize winner Edward Albee, who included her play *Funnyhouse of a Negro* as part of his Playwrights Workshop, which appeared off-Broadway in 1964. In the play, an African American woman named Sarah struggles with her identity and race. Sarah is torn apart by self-hate and alienation. Critics either praised the honesty and experimental form of the play or labeled the subject matter confusing. Yet *Funnyhouse* won Kennedy a prestigious Obie Award and placed her at the forefront of young dramatists of the 1960s.

The Rise of Female Black Poets

From its inception, the Black Arts movement was dominated by strong male voices and visions. Women, such as Kennedy, while not exactly discouraged from participating, often found themselves in secondary roles.

If the Black Arts movement had a matriarch, it may have been Gwendolyn Brooks.

Born in Topeka, Kansas, in 1917, she spent the majority of her childhood in Chicago. She published her first poem, "Eventide," at 13 in the popular children's magazine *American Childhood*, and at 17, she was regularly publishing poems in the *Chicago Defender*. After attending Wilson Junior College, Brooks became a homemaker and a poet. Her first collection of poems, *A Street in Bronzeville*, was published in 1945, 20 years before the Black Arts movement began. She experimented with language and wrote of

Gwendolyn Brooks was a major influence on writers who participated in the Black Arts movement.

gang life—life she had only observed from afar. Still, Brooks wrote with authenticity and understanding, and her words echoed the frustration of a whole generation. When Black Power came to prominence, she was ready for it. Writing poems about Malcolm X and encouraging younger writers to stand up for what they believed in, Gwendolyn Brooks set an example of strength and honor that the Black Arts movement deeply respected. In 1950, she was the first African American awarded the Pulitzer Prize.

In the late 1960s, black poets Nikki Giovanni and Sonia Sanchez, in particular, helped broaden the perspective of the movement. Taking inspiration from jazz music, poems became jagged, elliptical, and improvisational. The European conventions of verse were gone, replaced by open, streetwise tones steeped in the language of the people. Poems voiced joy, sadness, pride, and outrage—but now, the voice was openly black, politically black.

Giovanni's early work was raw, outraged at the state of blackness in America. In her 1968 poem "The True Import of Present Dialogue: Black vs. Negro," she prescribed a remedy, writing that a derogatory view of African American men must be killed and replaced by black men who are defined by responsibility, engagement, and pride. Sonia Sanchez's 1969 poem "blk/rhetoric" spoke of finding new heroes for African Americans, ones who would not simply use culture and greed as ways of making money.

Nikki Giovanni took inspiration from jazz music for her poems.

BLACK ART COLLECTIVES

Several black art collectives, such as the Spiral collective, AfriCOBRA, Kamoinge, and Weusi Artist Collective, began during the 1960s. These collectives were made up of African American artists who would gather together to talk about politics, art, and how they could effect change in their communities through art and activism.

On July 5, 1963, the Spiral collective was formed by Romare Bearden, Charles Alston, Norman Lewis, and Hale Woodruff. The artists in this group, which mostly consisted of painters, would meet at Bearden's loft to discuss their engagement in the civil rights movement; however, they all had differing views on what exactly that should be. This group organized one exhibition titled *First Group Showing: Works in Black and White*, which opened on May 14, 1965, and ran until June 5, 1965.

AfriCOBRA was a collective initially formed by artists Jeff Donaldson, Wadsworth Jarrell, Jae Jarell, Barbara Jones-Hogu, and Gerald Williams in Chicago in 1968. The members of this collective would often meet at the home and studio of Wadsworth and Jae Jarrell where they would discuss how they could use their art as a service to the black liberation movements. Before forming AfriCOBRA, many of its members were known for their contribution to creating the urban mural titled the *Wall of Respect*, which is located on Chicago's South Side and is a commemoration of black revolutionaries.

The style of Sanchez's and Giovanni's work was influenced, too, by the oral traditions of black ancestors. During slavery, blacks' only connection to their African past was through stories passed along by word of mouth from generation to generation. The new/old language used in poetry of the black arts was a look forward and a look back, crafted to be shouted or sung to an audience gathered for the sharing of ideas.

Other black female poets who contributed their poetry to the Black Arts movement included Audre Lorde, Jayne Cortez, June Jordan, Carolyn Rodgers, and Mari Evans. Without all of these women speaking their minds through their poetry, the movement would have been a mouthpiece solely spoken through by men. Their contributions helped to shape the female voice surrounding the Black Arts

The art collective Kamoinge, made up of two black photography groups, was formed in 1963 in Harlem. They were a group that was trying to help each other get their works exposed: "We saw ourselves as a group who were trying to nurture each other," Louis Draper, a cofounder of the collective, said in an interview with photography scholar Erina Duganne. "The magazines wouldn't support our work. So we wanted to encourage each other."[1] At first, the members of the group would hold meetings at each other's homes, then in 1965, they rented out the first floor of a brownstone in Harlem, which they called the Kamoinge Gallery. Here they would host workshops, share critiques, and welcome guest speakers and new members. "We wanted to show a picture that did not emphasize the negativity that the white photographers clung to when shooting in our community," Shawn Walker, a founding member of Kamoinge, said. "We could decide what images went into print."[2]

Weusi Artist Collective was an organization of African American artists, which formed in 1965 in Harlem. Some of the founding members of this group were Ben Jones, Otto Neals, Taiwo DuVall, Ademola Olugebefola, Okoe Pyatt, and Emmett Wigglesworth, among others. Their collective rejected artistic traditions and instead specifically created art that invoked African themes and symbols as a way to pay tribute to their heritage.

1. Quoted in Ashawnta Jackson, "When the White Establishment Ignored These Black Photographers, the Kamoinge Collective Was Born," Timeline, March 14, 2018. timeline.com/black-photographers-founded-the-kamoinge-collective-40dfa3eb4015.

2. Quoted in Jackson, "When the White Establishment Ignored These Black Photographers."

movement and would inspire many female artists who came after them.

Taking Their Independence Back

If African Americans were to be self-sufficient and independent from the white world and reconnect with their own heritage, then "a main tenet of Black Power is the necessity for Black people to define the world in their own terms,"[30] Larry Neal wrote. The taking of African names was only one part of this process.

Also essential to this transformation of self was a deeper commitment to the community in which a person lived, worked, and raised a family. However, for a race of people long dominated and discriminated against by a powerful white society, such commitment was by no means a given.

A RAISIN IN THE SUN

Lorraine Hansberry's 1959 play *A Raisin in the Sun* took its title from the Langston Hughes poem "Harlem," sometimes referred to as "A Dream Deferred." In addition to being the first black woman to write a Broadway play, she hired Lloyd Richards, a black director.

Hansberry's production starred Sidney Poitier, the first black actor to be nominated for a competitive Academy Award for *The Defiant Ones* in 1958. Despite not winning this first time, he later won the Academy Award for Best Actor for *Lilies of the Field* in 1963, which made him the first black actor to win the award in this category.

A Raisin in the Sun centers on the Younger family, taking place within the confines of their small apartment. There the family waits for a $10,000 life insurance check to arrive. Once it does, matriarch Lena puts a down payment on a home in a white neighborhood so her family will have a better life, and conflict ensues.

Unlike her main characters, Hansberry grew up in a wealthy family, but she saw firsthand the difficult bargains African Americans were often asked to make in white America. Hansberry dreamed of creating characters that broke black stereotypes, not reinforced them. It took producer Philip Rose more than a year to raise the required funds for a Broadway run, but *Raisin*'s success was

Local leadership was necessary to jump-start this new vision and establish a more self-reliant community. Black writer and publisher Haki R. Madhubuti spoke of a need for more independent black institutions, such as community centers, churches, and black-owned and operated businesses. Despite the many financial and organizational challenges, Madhubuti proved it could be done. From its inception, his Third World Press pledged to give back to the community. To this end, in 1969, Third World Press created the Institute for Positive Education, which held lectures, ran a bookstore, and showed films.

However, Third World's institute was only the beginning, as black communities throughout the United States built organizations, artistic and otherwise, for the promotion of African American values and ideas. In 1967, critic George Breitman recognized this local and national revolution in the making and wrote about the need for such black

immediate, both critically and commercially. The play also drew a new audience to Broadway. "Black people had not been attending the theater that much previously. It wasn't about them. And here was a play that was about them,"[1] Richards said.

Lorraine Hansberry is most well-known for writing the play A Raisin in the Sun.

At first, they took their play on the road. After raising enough money and receiving good reviews for their performances, they were offered a Broadway theater to showcase the play. The Broadway debut for *A Raisin in the Sun* took place at the Ethel Barrymore Theatre on March 11, 1959, later transferring to the Belasco Theatre. In 1961, it was made into a film starring most of the cast from the play.

1. Quoted in "*A Raisin in the Sun*," NPR, *Morning Edition*, March 11, 2002. www.npr.org/templates/story/story. hp?storyId=1139687.

institutions in the article "In Defense of Black Power." He praised Malcolm X for his fearless independence. He viewed the movement and Malcolm X as kindred spirits, and he described the movement's struggle against colonialism and the war brewing in Vietnam. Like Malcolm X, Breitman neither recommended violence nor discouraged it. He wrote that the movement "spurns the straitjacket of 'nonviolence' and proclaims the right of self-defense."[31]

The Black Arts Movement Is Born

By 1965, the straitjacket Breitman wrote about was ripped away. Unlike the Red Summer of 1919, the riots of 1965 were sparked by deep-seated frustration and anger on the part of African Americans. Neighborhoods such as Los Angeles and nearby Watts in California witnessed all-out guerrilla warfare, fires, and looting, or stealing goods.

African American artists, along with the rest of the nation, could only watch helplessly as the erupting violence took on a life of its own. Yet their writing would eventually reflect what they saw as they worked to turn the racial tensions into explosive poetry and drama.

The Watts riots, especially, became a symbol of the racial upheaval being felt everywhere in the mid-1960s. On August 11, 1965, when highway patrol officer Lee Minikus pulled over Marquette Frye, he suspected the black young man of being drunk. As Frye and his brother Ronald were questioned, a crowd of almost 300 people gathered. Rocks and garbage were thrown at Minikus and the other officers who had arrived to lend support. Before long, Rena Frye, Marquette's mother, arrived. During the incident, the rumor that the police had assaulted Marquette's mother and pregnant girlfriend circulated among the crowd. Due to the already volatile relationship between the police and African American community, combined with the hot weather, a scuffle ensued, and all three family members were arrested.

The arrests only ignited the tensions between police and Watts citizens, many of whom broke store windows, fired guns, and destroyed private property. The riots lasted for six days. In the end, the National Guard arrived to quell the unrest, however, 34 people died, 25 of them black, and more than 1,000 were injured. Police arrested 4,000 people. Nearly a thousand buildings were destroyed or damaged. Cost to the city and its taxpayers exceeded $40 million.

Interviewed in 2005, retired officer Minikus had no regrets. "I would do exactly what I did at the time,"[32] he said. In later years, Minikus and Marquette Frye became friends.

Like Minikus, Watts resident Tommy Jacquette was convinced he did the right thing. In his sixties, Jacquette took issue with those who call what happened in Watts a riot: "We call it a revolt," he said, "because it had a legitimate purpose. It was a response to police brutality and social exploitation of a community and of a people ... I think any time people stand up for their rights, it's worth it."[33]

Another riot that occured was the 1967 Detroit riot. It began after police raided an illegal after-hours drinking club that was having a welcome-home party for two returning Vietnam War veterans. Out of all those in attendance at the party, 82 African Americans were arrested. Many residents who witnessed the incident began protesting, vandalizing property, looting businesses, and starting fires. These protests began to spread to other areas of the city and the police lost control of the riots, which lasted for five days. In the end, the riots resulted in 43 deaths, including 33 African Americans and 10 whites.

The public's opinions about police brutality against black people were echoed in the music and poetry of the time. In his poem "Black Art," Baraka argued for brutal, take-no-prisoners poetry that took on the police and held them accountable for their unjust actions. Baraka wrote this poem in 1965 after the assassination of Malcolm X. It is one of two poems that sparked the beginning of the Black Arts movement in poetry. The poem stressed the importance of the black voice within black poetry. It emphasized why black poets should write from their own experiences, instead of trying to emulate white poets because it was their stories that were the ones being shut out. Another poem titled "The Black Arts Movement," written by Neal also contributed to the inception of this new revolution for black artists.

While there were many race riots during the 1960s that caused tragic results, these riots symbolized a bigger issue, which was the segregation and inequality between blacks and whites, and the mistreatment of black people at that time. Even though laws had been passed by the government that were supposed to make life easier for black people, those who opposed the passing of these laws continued to make things difficult for them. As tensions grew, black people continued to put up a fight for their rights. During this time, the Black Arts movement allowed black artists to express their real thoughts and emotions on discrimination, even in the midst of social progress.

CHAPTER THREE
GROUNDBREAKING CULTURAL INFLUENCERS

One of the first trailblazing artists to be associated with the Black Arts movement, and to influence its evolution, was Amiri Baraka in 1965. He brought a voice to the black artistic vision in his poetry and plays. He and others associated with Black Arts sought to incorporate the whole of black experience into their work, including the connection to Africa itself.

This idea was not a new one. The philosophy of Pan-Africanism—embraced by many in the Black Arts movement—focuses not on the differences of the African peoples but on what unites them and promotes unity against governments worldwide that seek to oppress Africans. The term itself, coined in the early 20th century, means "all Africanism."

Noted writer and sociologist W.E.B. Du Bois has been called the father of Pan-Africanism. According to historian Manning Marable, Du Bois's book *The Souls of Black Folk*, published

W.E.B. Du Bois was known as the father of Pan-Africanism.

in 1903, "helped to create the intellectual argument for the black freedom struggle in the twentieth century."[34] Pan-Africanism promoted resistance to imperialism, in which a dominating country overwhelmed a smaller, less powerful one. In the 1960s, the Black Arts movement would use similar language to describe white America's control of blacks.

First World Festival of Negro Arts

Less than 10 years before the Black Arts movement came to prominence, the push for a deeper understanding of Africa and its relation to people of color throughout the world gained new traction. In the late 1950s, the American Society of African Culture called for an arts summit. After much planning, the World Festival of Negro Arts opened in the West African nation of Senegal in 1966. The festival, which was founded by Senegal's first president Léopold Sédar Senghor, was considered the first of its kind and showcased the work of black artists from all over the world. An exhibit of Nigerian art was held in the town hall of the capital city, Dakar. Senegalese painter Iba N'Diaye's canvases were presented, and a filmmaking prize was awarded to director Ousmane Sembène for the first full-length film by an African, *La Noire de…*, which

is the film's French title. The English title for the film is *Black Girl*. The venues for the festival housed 2,500 artists and 25,000 attendees. Honored guests included American composer and bandleader Duke Ellington, poets Langston Hughes and Aimé Césaire, and dancer Alvin Ailey. Organizers described the festival as a celebration of African culture, a culture whose impact was now being felt worldwide.

"It successfully showcased the very real achievements of blacks in the world of arts and letters, along with their unique contributions to jazz, blues, and spirituals … The festival provided an extraordinary venue for black artists to demonstrate their achievements before a world audience,"[35] scholar Tracy D. Snipe said.

The Black Arts movement, too, celebrated African culture. Black citizens throughout the country had begun dressing in traditional African clothing and using traditional African names. However, despite an allegiance to their homeland, some African Americans—including many artists—were skeptical of the festival's purpose.

It was widely known that the U.S. government funded the festival. Black Arts leaders viewed the 1966 Festival of Negro Arts as a way for President Lyndon B. Johnson to push his civil rights program by portraying blacks

BLACK DANCE COMPANIES

Another art form that progressed during the Black Arts movement was dance. The most prominent dance groups formed were Alvin Ailey American Dance Theater, Dayton Contemporary Dance Company, the Dance Theatre of Harlem, the Philadelphia Dance Company (or Philadanco), Garth Fagan Dance, the Cleo Parker Robinson Dance Ensemble, and the Joel Hall Dancers. All of these dance companies specialized in African American dance; however, today, their members are of many races.

Thomas Gale wrote of the connection between dance and African culture: "Unlike the literary artists and theorists of the [black arts movement], whose acquaintance with Africa was too often only through cursory reading and vigorous fantasy, dancers had a highly developed tradition of African dance technique to draw upon."[1]

The most significant and influential of all these companies is Alvin Ailey American Dance Theater, which was founded in 1958 by choreographer and dancer Alvin Ailey. The group of black modern dancers first performed at New York City's 92nd Street Young Men's Hebrew Association. In 1962, he changed his all-black dance company into a multi-racial group. Some of Ailey's most famous works include *Revelations* (1960), *Night Creature* (1974), and *Cry* (1971). Ailey lost his battle with HIV/AIDS at age 58 in 1989. The dance company still operates under artistic director Robert Battle and the associate artistic director Masazumi Chaya.

1. Thomson Gale, "Black Arts Movement," *Encyclopedia of African-American Culture and History*, accessed on May 30, 2019. www.encyclopedia.com/history/biographies/historians-miscellaneous-biographies/black-aesthetic-movement.

Alvin Ailey is one of the most well-known dance companies in the world.

as less threatening than many whites believed they were. One American diplomat said as much by claiming the festival was meant to demonstrate "that Negroes are genuine participants in the 'mainstream' of 20th century American life" and "to demonstrate the interest of the United States in Negro and African art."[36]

Black Arts writer Larry Neal was also skeptical of the government's motives. Neal wrote:

> *Hundreds of artists of African descent came to what could have been a most significant event. Only, they found that it was constructed to attract everyone but Black people. The performances were attended by ninety-percent European and American whites; while the bulk of the Senegalese people either could not afford the festival, or were somehow discouraged from going.*[37]

Fanon Fighting Colonialism

The World Festival of Negro Arts brought the plight of non-American blacks into sharper focus. By then, members of the Black Arts movement, especially, began speaking out against colonialism in the developing world, most notably in Africa. The continent was prevalent with examples of peoples of color dominated by European nations. The growing awareness of racism and oppression throughout the world inspired black artists as never before.

In 1961, a study of colonialism sent shock waves through the black community. *The Wretched of the Earth*, written by Frantz Fanon, was a call to arms. The cover of the 1968 edition of the book recognized it as "The Handbook for the Black Revolution That Is Changing the Shape of the World."[38]

Early in the book, Fanon compares the colonists' town with that belonging to the colonized people. In his description, the artists and intellectuals of the Black Arts movement recognized their own inner cities:

> *The settlers' (colonists') town is a strongly built town, all made of stone and steel.*

> *It is a brightly lit town; the streets are covered with asphalt, and the garbage cans swallow all the leavings ... The settler's feet ... are protected by strong shoes although the streets of his town are clean and even, with no holes or stones.*

The Negro village ... is a place of ill fame, peopled by men of evil repute ... It is a world without spaciousness; men live there on top of each other ... The native town is a hungry town, starved of bread, of meat, of shoes, of coal, of light.[39]

Fanon himself came from a middle-class family on the island nation of Martinique. His early life afforded him a front-row seat to the hardship, poverty, and utter despair associated with colonialism. For centuries, Great Britain and France had fought over his country. In 1925, the year of Fanon's birth, France controlled it, and still does to this day.

During World War II, Fanon had loyally fought in the Free French Army to free France from Nazi control and remained there to study medicine and psychiatry at the University of Lyon once the war ended. During these years, Fanon began writing down his thoughts on being a black intellectual in a white man's world. He became interested in the mental burdens put on the colonized person like himself by the ruling country. It was a confusing existence, he admitted. He considered himself French, but he found racism among white Frenchmen hard to accept. The lack of hope experienced by so many oppressed people was, Fanon believed, related to this sense of confusion and conflicted sense of loyalty.

Such ideas were only reinforced during Fanon's next call to action. In 1954, the North African nation of Algeria, also a colony of France, was rocked by civil war. French colonies were legally considered French soil. Algeria's native Arabs, led by the National Liberation Front (NLF), revolted against French rule. The violence of the uprising shocked many French citizens. The NLF carried out bombings on a regular basis, resulting in mass casualties. The French government retaliated with harsh measures, including the torture and execution of suspected rebels and the murder of innocents. Fanon moved to Algeria to aid the Arab rebels. During one mission, he was severely wounded in Morocco in 1961. After entering a hospital in Rome, he was later moved to Bethesda, Maryland, where he died in December of that year.

However, before his death, Fanon proposed a solution to colonialism. In *The Wretched of the Earth*, he imagined a new world, one where the word "white" no longer signified good and "black" no longer signified evil, as in the past. This new world, he said, would come at a price: Only through violent revolution could it be achieved. "Violence is a cleansing force," he wrote.

"It frees the native from his inferiority complex and from his despair and inaction; it makes him fearless and restores his self-respect."[40]

Fanon's ideas were deeply influenced by Marxism. Derived directly from the work of 19th-century German philosophers Karl Marx and Friedrich Engels, Marxism highlighted the contributions of the working people, called the proletariat. The Marxist idea that history is the story of class struggle—the powerful versus the oppressed and exploited—changed the thinking of many in the Black Arts movement. Fanon's Marxist interests and support for the use of force gave voice to what so many in the Black Power and Black Arts movements strongly believed: The only way to achieve power was to take it.

In the coming years, Black Arts reflected this push for armed revolution. Through poems, plays, and musical expression, artists demanded recognition of their struggle and their past; whites had no choice but to acknowledge both the pain and the beauty of the African American journey.

"The New Thing"

The Black Arts movement required a new language to express itself. The old forms would no longer do. Harlem Renaissance writers had borrowed much of their form and style from the blues, but the younger generation needed a contemporary structure that would help convey its uniquely political and subversive image.

In 1963, LeRoi Jones—before changing his name—published a revolutionary look at the roots of music in the United States. *Blues People: Negro Music in White America* remains a central study of the connection between a people and an art form. Jones's work traced the origins of black music. Along the way, the author made important discoveries. "As I began to get into the history of the music, I found that this was impossible without ... getting deeper into the history of the people,"[41] Jones wrote.

By the time of his writing, it was clear that the major beneficiaries of black music were whites. While the forms were African American, artists like Elvis Presley and Jerry Lee Lewis sold millions of records and made millions of dollars by bringing traditionally black music to the white masses.

Yet despite the co-opting of rock and roll, one form of American music remained steeped in the language of black culture: jazz. Like the moon, art shifts and works its way through many phases over time. In the late 1950s, as a new black consciousness was beginning to grow in cities across the country, jazz musicians looked for new ways to express the times. World War II had ended more than a decade before. Black artists would no longer be boxed in by European forms of expression; neither were they completely satisfied with the bebop jazz of pioneers such as Miles Davis, Charlie Parker, and Dizzy Gillespie.

Upon his arrival in New York City in 1959, alto saxophonist Ornette Coleman announced that jazz must be "free," and for him, this meant, according to historian Geoffrey C. Ward, "employing strange scales, filled with vocalized smears and cries, seemingly unrelated either to a recognizable theme or to anything going on around him."[42] Free jazz, also known as "the new thing," confused many listeners, including other musicians, but Coleman was committed to breaking new ground and following his own musical muse: "The theme you play at the start of the number is the territory, and what comes after, which may have very little to do with it, is the adventure."[43]

Another jazz giant was saxophonist John Coltrane. Before superstardom, Coltrane had played with some of the best musicians of the time, including Davis. However, by 1962, Coltrane, who was famously obsessive about his work, was paving his own legendary path. When his wife, Alice, was out, Coltrane ignored phone calls and knocks at the door. He was compulsive about playing, just as he had been about drugs and alcohol in years past.

In 1957, Coltrane had been fired from Miles Davis's group because of his erratic behavior and addictions. Dejected, Coltrane returned to his home in Philadelphia and one day decided to change his life. "I experienced," he later wrote, "by the grace of God, a spiritual awakening which was to lead me to a richer, fuller, more productive life."[44] Coltrane turned his life around and poured his newfound devotion into his instrument. In 1964, he recorded the album *A Love Supreme*, an exploration of love for and faith in God. In writing about the work, Coltrane could have been speaking for many black artists who viewed their art as a force for change: "My music is the spiritual expression of what I am—my faith, my knowledge, my being ... When you begin to see the possibilities of music, you desire to do something really good for people, to help humanity free itself from its hangups ... I want to speak to their souls."[45]

While Coltrane was never directly involved with the Black Arts movement, he was deeply engaged in the plight of African Americans and deeply respected both Martin Luther King Jr. and Malcolm X, according to his second wife Alice: "He was very

Miles Davis (left) and John Coltrane (right) played jazz music together before Coltrane was fired from Davis's group in 1957.

interested in the civil-rights movement ... He did see the unity in what they were trying to achieve, basically almost the same thing, taking different directions to reach that point of achievement."[46] Baraka put it another way: "Malcolm told it like it was, and [Coltrane] played it like it was—hot and illuminating!"[47]

Yet Coltrane refused to become militant, instead preferring to use his music to change hearts and souls and uplift people. Still, Coltrane's record label, Impulse, recorded many musicians with a more politically charged approach, including Pharoah Sanders, Sun Ra, and Albert Ayler, all of whom had played many Sundays at the now-defunct Black Arts Repertory Theatre.

The music of the more militant members of the jazz community provided the soundtrack for the revolution and convinced more African Americans that change was essential, even inevitable. However, other black institutions would have to be transformed as well.

Impact of the Black Church

African American artists and thinkers wanted to alter the definition of what it meant to be black in America. To do this, old European-based images and beliefs had to be destroyed and white supremacy torn from its foundation, piece by piece. If the Black Arts movement used language, music, and images to reorder the world, then other black institutions were also intent on transformation.

For many African Americans, the church was the center of the community, the place people went for renewal and sanctuary. Yet in 1963, during the height of the civil rights movement, the 16th Street Baptist Church in Birmingham, Alabama, was bombed, killing four little girls. After this horrific event, rioting followed with Birmingham police shooting another black child. A white mob also pulled a young black man off of his bicycle and beat him to death in the street. These events—the senseless murder of innocents—riveted the nation. "I suddenly realized what it was to be black in America," said singer and pianist Nina Simone. "It came as a rush of fury, hatred and determination. In church language, the Truth entered into me."[48]

What entered Albert Cleage's mind in Detroit in the late 1960s was the realization that even the basic rituals and symbols of faith were steeped in tyranny and racism. Cleage, leader of the black theology movement, who would later change his name to Jaramogi Abebe Agyeman in the early 1970s, used his church as a place for new ideas about what it meant to be a person of faith. His innovations became one more example of a cultural conversion that would have a profound impact on the way black people viewed themselves.

First, Cleage renamed his church the Shrine of the Black Madonna. Convinced that oppression and self-worth were linked, Cleage had traditionally white religious figures, including Jesus and his mother, Mary, painted with darker complexions. "White supremacy was so powerful," wrote scholar Peniel E. Joseph, "that even the religious figures blacks looked to for eternal salvation were white."[49]

Cleage referred to contemporary religious practices as "slave Christianity" and worked to tie religion to the ongoing black revolution: "From the pulpit he cast Jesus as the Black Messiah," Joseph said. "Envisioning Jesus as a proud and radical black prophet who raged against political and economic oppression."[50]

Cleage was outspoken and militant on matters of white domination, but he also did not spare his own people. He spoke of "how good blacks were at tearing things up,"[51] but seemed unwilling to build communities and institutions.

Yet religion was not the only facet of life in which many blacks saw the heavy and dispiriting influence of whites. Before his death, Malcolm X had drawn a stark distinction between the "black revolution" and the "Negro revolution."[52] The Negro revolution, embodied artistically in the Harlem Renaissance and politically in the civil rights movement of Martin Luther King Jr., had made little progress for black people, he said. Malcolm X continued, "Whoever heard of a revolution where they lock arms, as Rev. Cleage was pointing out beautifully, singing 'We Shall Overcome'? You don't do that in a revolution. You don't do any singing, you're too busy swinging."[53]

Opposing Sides

While Malcolm X had previously disagreed with King's stance on how to achieve equality for blacks among whites during the civil rights movement, he came to somewhat appreciate King's perspective after the two met on Capitol Hill. Both men only met once when they were alive and it was on March 26, 1964, during a Senate debate regarding legislation aimed at ending segregation in public places and racial discrimination in the workplace. President John F. Kennedy had put this bill into place after the insistence of King, and it was later pushed through to Congress by President Lyndon B. Johnson.

That day, as King stepped out of a press conference, Malcolm X approached King and they shook hands. While their exchange only lasted a minute, he told King, "I'm throwing myself into the heart of the civil rights struggle."[54] Four days later, opponents of the bill launched one of the longest filibusters in U.S. history to try to prevent the bill from passing.

In April of that year, Malcolm X visited North Africa and the Middle East, and while he was there, his perspective on race in America changed ever so slightly. Although he did not fully abandon his previous beliefs, he came to see how peace rather than violence helped African Americans. "I was no less angry than I had been, but at the same time the true brotherhood I had seen had influenced me to recognize that anger can blind human vision," Malcolm X said after visiting those parts of the world.

NINA SIMONE

Eunice Kathleen Waymon, who would later become known as the famous singer Nina Simone, was born in Tryon, North Carolina, on February 21, 1933. At the age of three, she began playing piano by ear. Growing up, she played piano in her mother's church. She began studying with an Englishwoman named Muriel Mazzanovich and grew to love all the classical pianists, such as Johann Sebastian Bach and Ludwig van Beethoven. After graduating as valedictorian from her high school, she traveled to Juilliard in New York City to study music. Then, she applied to the prestigious Curtis Institute of Music in Philadelphia. However, she was denied admission. She would maintain that the reason for her rejection was due to her race.

In 1954, Waymon auditioned to sing at the Midtown Bar & Grill on Pacific Avenue in Atlantic City, New Jersey. It was here that she would transform into Nina Simone—a way to disguise herself from family members, as her mother claimed she was "working in the fires of hell."[1] She was known for transforming popular songs into a unique blend of jazz, blues, and classical music.

She would eventually record George Gershwin's "I Loves You, Porgy" from the opera *Porgy and Bess*, which became her only top 20 success in the United States. At age 24, she was discovered by the recording industry and was signed by Syd Nathan's Jazz imprint Bethlehem Records. She released her debut album *Little Girl Blue* in 1958.

During the civil rights movement and Black Arts movement, Simone became an activist and used her music to fuel the messages behind these movements. In 1964, she released a protest song "Mississippi Goddam," which was her response to the 1963 murder of Medgar Evers in Mississippi and, in that same year, the 16th Street Baptist Church bombing in Birmingham, Alabama, that killed four black children. The song was banned in several Southern states with boxes of the records returned from radio stations cracked in half. In March 1965, she performed the song before tens of thousands of marchers in Selma, Alabama, on a stage propped up by coffins. In a clip from the 2015 documentary *What Happened, Miss Simone?*, comedian and activist Dick Gregory said: "If you look at all the suffering black folks went through, not one black man would dare say 'Mississippi Goddam.' We all wanted to say it. She said it."[2] Some of her other famous protest songs include "Four Women" and "To Be Young, Gifted and Black."

Singer and pianist Nina Simone was a dedicated activist during the civil rights movement and Black Arts movement.

1. Quoted in "Bio," Estate of Nina Simone, accessed on April 5, 2019. www.ninasimone.com/bio/.

2. Quoted in Adam Chandler, "What Happened to Nina Simone?," *The Atlantic*, June 27, 2015. www.theatlantic.com/entertainment/archive/2015/06/nina-simone-and-mississippi-goddam/396923/.

Martin Luther King Jr. and Malcolm X only met each other once—in 1964.

He added, "America is the first country... that can actually have a bloodless revolution."[55]

On July 2, 1964, the Civil Rights Act of 1964, which outlawed discrimination based on race, color, religion, sex, or national origin, was signed into law. This law gave hope to both King and Malcolm X; however, they both would only be around a short time after it passed. Despite their deaths, they left legacies highlighting their dedicated work to the movement of making the world a better place for black people to live in, and this would inspire many more who would serve as advocates and leaders of this revolution.

CHAPTER FOUR
TO CONFORM OR NOT TO CONFORM?

Three days after the assassination of Martin Luther King Jr. in 1968, Nina Simone and her band played a heartfelt tribute for the reverend at the Westbury Music Festival in Long Island, New York. The song, titled "Why? (The King of Love is Dead)," was composed by Simone's bass player Gene Taylor on April 5, 1968, the day after King was murdered at the Lorraine Motel in Memphis, Tennessee.

Simone knew it was time to react to the continued prejudice against black people that had become widespread throughout America. Some of the lyrics in the tribute song helped her to express why this was such a crucial time for the black community to band together and demand respect and equality.

As the 1960s drew to a close, black leaders and citizens wrestled with the primary issue of their generation: Should they assimilate with white culture or walk the path of self-determination? The Black Power and Black Arts movements knew their answer. The murder of Martin Luther King Jr. was a tragic reminder of a brutal truth: Some whites would rather kill than allow a place for blacks at America's table.

Three years after his death, Malcolm X's message of self-defense resonated with more African Americans than ever before; in short order, an organization based on his principles of black nationalism would rise. The Black Arts movement would play a vital role in taking that controversial message to the streets of America's cities.

Art and Politics
In 1966, less than two years after the Black Arts Repertory Theatre fell apart over internal struggles and a lack of funding, LeRoi Jones divorced his first wife, Hettie Cohen, and married poet Sylvia Robinson (who later changed

53

her name to Amina Baraka). Soon after, Jones changed his name—a reflection, apparently, of his deeper commitment to black culture and his African ancestry. Taking the name Imamu (or spiritual leader) Amiri Baraka, the preeminent figure of the Black Arts movement served notice on white America. Although he would later drop "Imamu," Baraka remained a key figure in the movement, but now he was only one part of it.

Baraka's friend Larry Neal kept writing too, becoming a bold voice and challenging old notions of black creativity and expression. "The Black Arts and the Black Power concept both relate broadly to the Afro-American's desire for self-determination and nationhood," Neal wrote in his influential essay "The Black Arts Movement." "One is concerned with the relationship between art and politics; the other with the art of politics."[56] To Neal, politics was an art—one that had been used to control and subjugate black people for generations. He believed that it was time for black artists and organizations to take back the power of the image and the word to spread a new message and rally the masses.

Pride and a sense of self-worth were the essential qualities of the message. First, black people must recognize their own uniqueness and beauty, as well as their ties to a rich and proud culture. If the U.S. government ignored their urban communities, African Americans would not. Instead, they would feed and educate their own people. In time, black people would even harness the power of the ballot box, electing representatives sympathetic to their needs. These goals were lofty but not out of reach. However, the system was broken. Black America needed a political vehicle for change—a group of men and women ready to lead it through the revolution.

Black Panther Party

In 1966, the Black Panther Party was founded by Bobby Seale and Huey Newton. Their original purpose was to patrol African American neighborhoods to protect residents from police brutality. During this time, through music and images, the Black Arts movement helped fashion a potent new vision of black aggression and determination. Many members of the movement, including Neal, joined the Panthers and helped raise money for legal defense funds.

Yet not all black artists were as supportive of the Black Arts movement and its politics. Poet and novelist Ishmael Reed was outspoken in his disdain for many elements of the movement. Reed, controversial and left-wing like Baraka, had been a member of the radical Umbra Writers Workshop in the early 1960s. Umbra forged the artistic foundation of the Black Arts movement through poetry readings and its namesake publication, and Reed's own work "affirmed various black cultures"[57] through the use of black folklore, according to author Jerry Gafio Watts.

Still, despite Reed's sympathy with many of the Black Arts movement's goals, he strongly criticized its ideas and methods, calling them a "goon squad aesthetic" and "tribalism ... for the birds."[58] For this, Reed found himself criticized by the black press.

Joe Goncalves, a strong supporter of the Black Arts movement and editor of the influential *Journal of Negro Poetry*, leveled harsh words at Reed, saying he was "always serving some white man's purpose."[59]

Such criticism only echoed the ongoing generational conflict developing between the older, more established black writers and this new group of intellectuals. For young advocates like Baraka and Neal, writers such as Ralph Ellison were ancient history; unable or simply unwilling to take the necessary next steps toward self-reliance and power.

Bobby Seale and Huey Newton founded the Black Panther Party in 1966.

FEMALES OF THE BLACK PANTHER PARTY

While many members of the Black Panther Party were men, there were also many influential women who were members of the party. Some of these women included Angela Davis, Elaine Brown, Kathleen Cleaver, Fredricka Newton, Charlotte Hill O'Neal, Assata Shakur, Afeni Shakur, Rosemari Mealy, Ericka Huggins, Barbara Easley Cox, and even the famous singer Chaka Khan. The Black Panther Party is known for its image of black men with guns monitoring the police force to ward off oppressors; however, it was the organization's female members who ensured the party's survival. As the 1970s came along, women made up the majority of the party, and today, many of these same women continue to fight for the rights of black people.

Brown was the first woman to head the organization from 1974 to 1977. Despite her high ranking in the organization, her feminist approach seemed to cause conflict within the Black Power movement, as she said: "A woman in the Black power movement was considered, at best, irrelevant. A woman asserting herself was a pariah. If a black woman assumed a role of leadership, she was said to be eroding black manhood, to be hindering the progress of the black race."[1]

In 1967, Davis joined the Black Panther Party while she was pursuing a master's degree from the University of California, San Diego. Eventually, she joined the all-black branch of the Communist Party and began pursuing prison reform advocacy in order to help free black prisoners, some of whom were Black Panthers. In 1970, Davis was arrested as the prime suspect in a case claiming she assisted a Black Panther in breaking out of a jail after guns were found registered in her name. This led to her name being on the FBI's most wanted list and launched the "Free Angela Davis" campaign. Despite law enforcement tarnishing her name, Davis gained support from several people, even famous ones, such as John Lennon, Yoko Ono, the Rolling Stones, and Aretha Franklin, who offered to pay her bail:

Angela Davis must go free. Black people will be free. I've been locked up ... and I know you got to disturb the peace when you can't get no peace. Jail is hell to be in. I'm going to see her free if there is any justice in our courts, not because I believe in communism, but because she's a black woman and she wants freedom for black people. I have the money; I got it from black people.[2]

Many people thought the practices of the Black Panther Party were violent and racist. However, former Black Panther David Hilliard said, "We did not practice racist ideology. The system was discriminatory and violent. Our slogan became revolution and survival, pending transformation of society; survival pending revolution."[3] Other than monitoring the police and promoting for black liberation, the party created free school breakfast programs for children, and also provided sickle cell anemia testing, legal aid, and adult education.

1. Quoted in Christina Coleman, "Black Panther 50 – Here Are the Women of the Black Panther Party," *Essence*, October 21, 2016. www.essence.com/holidays/black-history-month/women-black-panther-party/.

2. Quoted in Sam Lefebvre, "How Aretha Franklin Supported Angela Davis and the Black Panthers," KQED, August 16, 2018. www.kqed.org/arts/13839139/how-aretha-franklin-supported-angela-davis-and-the-black-panthers.

3. Quoted in DeNeen L. Brown, "'I Have All the Guns and Money': When a Woman Led the Black Panther Party," *Washington Post*, January 10, 2018. www.washingtonpost.com/news/retropolis/wp/2018/01/09/i-have-all-the-guns-and-money-when-a-woman-led-the-black-panther-party/.

After Angela Davis was arrested in 1970, people protested her arrest claiming it was unjust.

As with so many new artistic movements—Romanticism, Naturalism, Modernism—the previous school of thought was labeled obsolete and out of step. To gain a foothold, the new movement had to destroy the old movement; from those ashes—and with the aid of new thinkers and new writers—a fresh aesthetic would rise and, perhaps, change things. This was the dream; the reality was far more complex.

Powerful Images

The Black Arts movement evolved, in large part, at the same time as the African American political organizations of the time. One of the more influential political groups of the 1960s was the Student Nonviolent Coordinating Committee, or SNCC. First organized in Raleigh, North Carolina, in response to civil rights sit-ins in 1960, SNCC was persistent in its efforts to gain black voters equal rights, among other things.

Barely recognized as an organization at the time, it had a profound effect on civil rights and eventually attracted more radical members. What SNCC realized early on was that images could inspire and sometimes frighten people. They were the first group to choose the black panther as a symbol of the struggle, but they would not be the last. The black public needed powerful visions of blackness. The ferocious panther, crouching and ready to strike, fit the bill perfectly. In time, the stealthy animal would adorn T-shirts, stickers, and banners across the country.

Such imagery was crucial, both for the Black Arts movement and for the communities it served, because it drew a distinction between whites and blacks. "The Black Arts Movement presupposes a separate symbolism,"[60] Neal said. However, black nationalists also needed actual human beings to embody the strength and fortitude they believed necessary to achieve their goals.

SNCC organizer Stokely Carmichael was a panther personified. During his years at Howard University, Carmichael traveled to the Deep South to register black voters. Racist southerners worked hard to keep African Americans from voting, but Carmichael and his SNCC coworkers often braved violence to get people to the polls.

Although SNCC remained a nonviolent organization, Carmichael questioned the intelligence of that stand. "I just don't see it as a way of life," he said, "I never have. I also realize that no one in this country is asking the white community in the South to be nonviolent, and that in a sense it is giving them a free license to shoot us at will."[61]

African Americans were also finding other ways to express their solidarity. Movie stars, musicians, singers, and even athletes began showing off their political sympathies. Another symbol of Black Power was the raised fist. Printed on posters, record albums, and books, it represented unity, strength, and the willingness to fight for what one believed in.

At the 1968 Summer Olympics in Mexico, star American runners Tommie Smith and John Carlos caused a bit of controversy. Upon winning the gold and bronze medals, respectively, Smith and Carlos bowed their heads and raised their black-gloved fists as the U.S. national anthem played. Smith explained what each part of his outfit symbolized: "I wore black gloves to represent social power or Black power. I wore socks without shoes to represent poverty. I wore a black scarf around my neck to symbolize the lynchings, the hangings that black folks went through while building this country."[62] Their actions on the podium landed them in deep trouble with the Olympic Committee, with a spokesperson calling the display "a deliberate and violent breach of the fundamental principles of the Olympic spirit."[63]

A year before the incident, Smith said black members of the Olympic team were considering a boycott of the games, but that never happened. Still, he said, "It is very discouraging to be in a team with white athletes. On the track you are Tommie Smith, the fastest man in the world, but once you are in the dressing rooms you are nothing more than a dirty Negro."[64]

In 2016, Colin Kaepernick, then a quarterback for the San Francisco 49ers, carried out a similar act of protest by kneeling during the playing of "The Star-Spangled Banner," during which players normally

After winning the gold and bronze medals, American runners Tommie Smith (center) and John Carlos (right) raised their fists in protest against racism in the United States.

RACE RIOTS INSPIRE ART

While race riots exploded across the country in the middle and late 1960s, artists, black and white, used the chaos and violence to inspire their work. In April of 1968, Canadian folk singer Gordon Lightfoot released "Black Day in July." The song, which was about the 1967 Detroit riot, was quickly banned on American radio. Radio stations "don't want to upset their listeners," said Lightfoot in an interview. "It's a housewife in the morning, you know, like let's give her something to make her happy. You know, I give something that's going to make her think."[1]

Other songs that were inspired by these riots included John Lee Hooker's "The Motor City is Burning" in 1967, the Temptations's "Ball of Confusion (That's What The World Is Today)" in 1970, and David Bowie's "Panic in Detroit" in 1973. Hooker, who lived in Detroit at the time of the riots, did not participate in the unrest but could see the smoke and fire from his home on Jameson Street:

> I know what they were fightin' for … I feel bitter about that. A big city like Detroit … you know, racial like that. It wasn't like Mississippi, but … they hide it under the cover there. In Mississippi they didn't hide it, they just come out with it, and that's the only difference. It finally got so hot, people got so fed up, that the riot broke out, with all the burnin' and the shootin', the killin'. I could just look at the fire from my porch or my window, outside in my yard … I could see places goin' up in flame, hear guns shootin', robbin' stores, runnin' the business people out of they stores. There was a lotta lootin' goin' on, y'know … the po-lice was even lootin'. They like to have burned the whole city down.[2]

In "Ball of Confusion," the Temptations reference "cities aflame in the summer time," and "white flight"[3] that resulted from the riots and racial tension.

stand. He explained his act of protest by saying, "I am not going to stand up to show pride in a flag for a country that oppresses black people and people of color. To me, this is bigger than football and it would be selfish on my part to look the other way. There are bodies in the street and people getting paid leave and getting away with murder."[65] He also said he would not

More recent works that were inspired by the panic in Detroit are the 2002 novel *Middlesex* by Jeffrey Eugenides and the 2017 Kathryn Bigelow-directed film *Detroit*. Eugenides' haunting prose captures the fear and helplessness of a city in flames and under fire:

> *Outside, they were at it again: the snipers ... Each night, the sinking sun, like a ring on a window shade, pulled night down over the neighborhood. From wherever the snipers disappeared to during the hot day, they returned. They took up their positions. From the windows of condemned hotels, from fire escapes and balconies, from behind cars jacked up in front yards, they extended the barrels of their assorted guns.*[4]

The film *Detroit* tells the true story of the riots in the summer of 1967 in Detroit. This film focuses on the three young African American men who were murdered at the Algiers Motel and the brutal beatings of nine others, which included seven black men and two white women.

John Lee Hooker's "The Motor City Is Burning" was inspired by the 1967 Detroit riots.

1. Quoted in "Gordon Lightfoot Banned in the U.S.A.," CBC Player, April 13, 1968. www.cbc.ca/player/play/1726194667.

2. Quoted in Charles Shaar Murray, "Cuttin' Heads: Motor City Is Burning," Louder, May 20, 2014. www.loudersound.com/features/cuttin-heads-motor-city-is-burning.

3. Quoted in Ben Solis, "6 Songs Inspired by Riot and Rebellion in Detroit, 1967," MLive, accessed on May 28, 2019. www.mlive.com/news/detroit/2017/07/6_songs_about_detroit_1967_fin.html.

4. Jeffrey Eugenides, *Middlesex*. New York, NY: Picador, 2002, p. 275.

return to standing until the "[American] flag represents what it's supposed to represent."[66] Several other NFL players supported Kaepernick's stance and kneeled during the national anthem as well. Once Kaepernick left the 49ers in 2016, he went unsigned as a player for the next season, which led to allegations that he was not being chosen for a team because of his on-field political statements. This led him to file a lawsuit, particularly a grievance for collusion against the owners of the NFL, in November 2017. In 2019, it was said that Kaepernick reached a confidential settlement with the NFL and he withdrew the grievance.

The Panthers Take Charge

Smith grew up in the inner city and knew what life was like there. Part of the reality for blacks living in American inner cities in the 1960s was police harassment and brutality. Poverty and mass unemployment frustrated a generation of young black men and women, and some turned to crime, which brought increased police presence. As mostly white police officers patrolled predominantly black neighborhoods of Harlem, New York, or West Philadelphia, Pennsylvania, or Oakland, California, tensions rose. The racism and misunderstanding that led to the riots in Watts and Detroit prevailed. Black people viewed law enforcement as a major part of the problem; law enforcement was stretched to the limit and quick to judge. This made for a lethal combination.

In 1966, when Seale and Newton formed the Black Panther Party for Self-Defense, their initial goal was to monitor the actions of police in their neighborhoods, but their ambitions soon grew. Carrying law books and machine guns, the Panthers called for armed revolution. Carmichael joined the party too, saying, "If we don't get justice we're going to tear this country apart."[67] These Panthers were not about following the orders of those in power; their angry rhetoric was matched by violent action. In two years of open conflict, 9 police officers were killed and 56 were wounded, as well as 10 Panthers killed. As far as the Black Panthers were concerned, only armed confrontation with those in power would help them attain their goals of separatism and justice.

The Black Panthers' look matched their demeanor, as they typically dressed in leather jackets, black berets, and dark glasses. Their militant look outraged some and excited others. For many, though, it was the attitude that accompanied the image that captivated. "The thing that I really loved about the Black Panthers is that they refused to be ignored,"[68] supporter Father George Clements said.

Numerous black artists also supported the Panthers and their tactics. Writer Neal joined one branch of the group. Baraka spoke at rallies and allied himself with their politics. His poetry had long reflected the aggressive rhetoric the Panthers now used to speak to their audiences.

The Black Arts movement became a mouthpiece for the passionate views and revolutionary spirit of the Black Panthers. Yet there were key differences, according to critic Mike Sell: "While the Panthers attempted to seduce and exploit the media ... by way of outrageous, blatant displays of hypermasculine 'Blackness,' the Black Arts Movement sought to evade the white media [and white traditions] ... by taking their revolutionary [ideas] ... to historically African American colleges and urban ... African American communities."[69] Furthermore, said Sell, "While the Panthers saw the benefits of art primarily as a means to an end [such as fund-raising], Black Artists viewed art—as they viewed African Americans themselves—as both the means and the end of revolution."[70]

Regardless of their differences, the two groups are linked because of their basic belief in black nationalism. Yet not all African Americans approved of the Panthers' tactics, or do today. "I question the whole purpose of the Black Panther Party," former defender William O'Neal said. "They were necessary. It was a shock treatment for white America to see black men running around with guns just like black men had saw white man running around with guns. Yeah, that was a shock treatment.

It was good in that extent. But it got a lot of black people hurt."[71] As for whites, the Panthers "symbolized ... the worsening threat of black violence in the United States," according to scholar Robert J. Norrell. "Whites generally perceived it as a direct challenge to law and order—and thus to their own security."[72]

Newton, one of the Panther leaders, defended his party and his criticism of the police. In at least one case, he framed the argument in almost artistic terms. "I knew that images had to be changed," he said. "I know ... that words, the power of the word, words stigmatize people. We felt that the police needed a label, a label other than that fear image that they carried in the community."[73] The word used by the Panthers to identify the police would stick: pigs.

Eldridge Cleaver

Times were changing, as African Americans were forcing whites to take them seriously. These calls for justice could be witnessed on the streets, in churches, and at public events. After all, African American dreams were American dreams, yet for so many years they were not treated like the rest of America.

Like many cities across the nation, San Francisco—across the bay from Oakland, the Black Panthers' hometown—was a hotbed of Black

Power activity. Panther Eldridge Cleaver, recently paroled from prison, took command of the organization after Huey Newton and Bobby Seale were jailed for their activities.

Aside from his abilities as a leader, Cleaver was also a gifted writer who wrote about his experiences with white oppression. He began writing in Folsom State Prison in 1958, after being convicted on an assault charge. His writings were first released in the magazine *Ramparts* in 1965. After his release from prison in 1966, his writings were turned into a book titled *Soul on Ice*, a memoir and collection of essays that became a best seller, selling more than a million copies. His work attracted many fans, including revolutionary writer James Baldwin. White intellectuals in particular hailed Cleaver's ideas as groundbreaking. Before the publication of his book, Cleaver had remained anonymous because of his past legal troubles; afterward, he became an instant celebrity and voice for the movement, at least for a time.

The First Black Studies Program

Cleaver got people's attention, as did San Francisco's Black House, which became the center of West Coast black nationalism. Playwright and poet Marvin X, formerly Marvin Jackmon, founded the organization with playwright Ed Bullins. Marvin X, connected for a time to the Nation of Islam, is best known for his play *Flowers for the Trashman*. The drama chronicles the struggles of a black intellectual in an educational system designed for whites.

Black House itself "doubled as Cleaver's primary residence [and] buzzed with activity," said writer Peniel E. Joseph, "welcoming artists, authors, and political activists."[74] Artists, such as Jones and Sanchez, connected with Black House, and many from other parts of the country stayed a while. The center of the revolution had switched coasts by 1968, especially after San Francisco State University took a bold step forward. The institution's Black Student Union voted to support a black studies program. This was the first time that such an educational program had been deemed acceptable by the academic elites.

However, acceptance did not come immediately. In fact, San Francisco State administration condemned the program as "an intellectual and political fraud,"[75] according to Joseph. Only through the intervention and teaching of Jones, Sanchez, and black nationalist poet Ronald Snellings did the black studies program gain a foothold.

Regardless of the initial success,

NATHAN HARE

While growing up in segregated Slick, Oklahoma, in 1933, Nathan Hare's ambition was to become a boxer. Although Hare would return to this passion in later years, the fighting spirit of his youth served him well throughout his entire life.

Hare's academic career began as a sociology professor at the historically black Howard University in 1961, where his students included activist Stokely Carmichael. In 1966, after criticizing Howard president James Nabrit for insisting that Howard's student body should be 60 percent white by 1970, Hare was fired. Two years later, San Francisco State College (now San Francisco State University) hired Hare to develop a black studies program, the first of its kind in the United States.

Beginning with the premise that academia was, by nature, biased toward the history and experiences of Caucasians, Hare and San Francisco State students composed the "Black University Manifesto."[1] The document called for an overthrow of black colleges based on white ideals—clearly a reference to Hare's former employer. In 1968, San Francisco State University became the first academic institution in the country to have a black studies department. Other important work followed, including Hare's founding of the *Black Scholar*, the most important black journal since *The Crisis*. One of Hare's primary goals, he wrote, was "to build in black youth a sense of pride."[2]

Nathan Hare started the first black studies program in the United States at San Francisco State University.

1. Quoted in "Hare, Nathan 1934–," Encyclopedia.com, accessed on June 17, 2019. www.encyclopedia.com/education/news-wires-white-papers-and-books/hare-nathan-1934.

2. Quoted in William L. Van Deburg, *Modern Black Nationalism: From Marcus Garvey to Louis Farrakhan.* New York, NY: New York University Press, 1997, p. 160.

black studies and the African American students who supported it with Black Panther–style tactics often ran into trouble with the conservative university administration. However, the fuse had been lit, and soon enough other campuses around the country were heeding the call. Black studies programs—some legitimate and some less so—sprang up almost everywhere.

Black artists led the charge, mingling with Black Panthers at rallies and writing poems of racial militancy. The Panthers and the poets were unifying as never before. According to Joseph, it was at this time that Jones (the future Baraka) was transformed. "In front of three hundred students and numerous television cameras," Joseph wrote, "Jones argued that the time had come for blacks to arm themselves."[76]

What they armed themselves with were strong words and a willingness to push back. Author Henry Louis Gates Jr. remembered the electricity coursing through the lecture halls of many major universities, including one in which he saw poet Nikki Giovanni give a reading. "Her words seemed incandescent with racial rage," he said, "and each poem was greeted with a Black Power salute. 'Right on! Right on!' we shouted, in the deepest voices we could manage, each

time Giovanni made another grand claim about the blackness of blackness."[77]

The righteous enthusiasm of Gates and other students throughout the nation ensured that black studies programs continued to flourish. They remain a vital part of the educational system at many colleges and universities today. The excitement and militancy such programs inspired in the late 1960s brought the ideas of the Black Power movement to cities and neighborhoods.

The Black Arts movement aided the larger movement by giving voice to the frustration, anger, and determination of an entire generation of young people. "There was ... a positive overall effect of the Black Arts concept that still remains," Baraka said. "We showed that we had heard and understood Malcolm and that we were trying to create an art that would be a weapon in the Black Liberation Movement."[78]

While strides were being made to promise the same rights and respect to black people as whites in the United States, there were still many obstacles to overcome. In the coming years, the emergence of more black artists expressing their innermost feelings about the racial push and pull in America would help in the effort to achieve this goal.

CHAPTER FIVE
THE MOVEMENT GOES MAINSTREAM

When the Black Arts movement began, it was not a movement that was heavily advertised to all communities—it started underground. It was established in people's homes, in corner cafes, and in university quads. It was a movement for black people to be welcomed by, encouraged by, and hopefully, one day, feel freed by. Those who were involved in the movement spread the word, attended cultural events, and even added their voices to the surging sense of empowerment. However, in time, what began as a radical fringe idea grew in stature and acceptance. Once black arts and black artists were discovered by mainstream America, everything changed.

Showcasing the All-Natural

For centuries, the image of American blacks was defined by white society. The beauty queens and movie stars on magazine covers and on TV screens were, with few exceptions, white. There were seldom examples of African Americans embracing their typical features—wider noses, thicker lips, or all-natural hair—in American media, while blonde hair and blue eyes became the all-American vision of perfection.

During the heyday of the Black Arts movement, poems, plays, and paintings began depicting African Americans as vibrant, strong, and beautiful. Despite the popularity and political relevance of the term, *black* was a misnomer. People of color came in all shades—some lighter, others darker. As for hair, the younger generation abandoned the close-cropped "do" or the lye-straightened conk of the past generation and grew their hair out into bush-like Afros. Many also took to wearing brightly patterned African shirts, blouses, and robes.

White Americans, as well as many black Americans, viewed these developments as a serious threat to their way of life. While African Americans were already immersed in white society, often competing with whites for jobs and other essential benefits, many people questioned these acts of nonconformity.

Famously, all-black Howard University found itself on the front line of the debate. In the early 1960s, Howard remained stuck in the past. This "Black Harvard" was conservative by the standards of the Black Power movement because its leaders felt it had to compete with its white counterparts. Generations of black doctors, lawyers, and other professionals received stellar educations at Howard, yet the question remained: Was Howard willing to step into the future, or would it cling to its proud, but old-school, traditions?

Although Black Power had been holding rallies around the country, Howard's administrators and many of its students seemed reluctant to join the bandwagon. "As a student leader, you felt like you were being pulled apart, pulled in different directions by what you thought the right way to deal with the problem was as opposed to what the popular opinions on campus happened to reflect,"[79] Howard alumnus Fred Black said.

In October 1966, five young women competed for the title of homecoming queen; only one of them, Robin Gregory, wore an Afro. "I felt it was real important at that time," Gregory said, "because the Black Power movement was new, that we as people begin to accept ourselves, you know, just as who we were."[80] Gregory and the five other women campaigned for two weeks for the title of homecoming queen. On the night of the announcement, as the stage lights dimmed in the auditorium, the audience waited in anticipation. Former Howard student Paula Giddings remembered: "You saw the silhouette of her afro before you saw her ... the auditorium exploded and everybody exploded."[81] Gregory's crowning as queen marked an immense change for Howard University and for the country at large. Not only could black be beautiful, but students with the style and politics of Black Power were also now being recognized.

"That's what we tried to change when we moved into the black arts, black culture, black consciousness movement," Sonia Sanchez said. "I said never again will I allow anyone to live and walk on the planet earth and not like what they are, what they've been."[82]

The Spirit of Soul

It is difficult to determine exactly who first used the word *soul* to describe a state of being. Jazz singer Billie Holiday had soul. Her rasp spoke of the drugs and alcohol she had abused; it also contained a road map to her life, written in the lyrics of great composers such as George Gershwin and Johnny Mercer.

Legendary singer Sam Cooke sang soul, but he also *had* soul. A generation after Holiday's heyday, Cooke's 1965 ballad "A Change Is Gonna Come" was of the moment and ancient at the same time—the musical equivalent of Langston Hughes's poem "A Negro Speaks of Rivers" decades before. The speaker is born near a river, and he, like the river itself, spends his life running. The song is melancholy but hopeful as he repeatedly croons how someday things will change.

Despite its connection to the past, soul seemed contemporary and new. It attested to what African Americans wore, how they walked, and the language they used to speak to one another. "To be soulful," Baraka wrote, "is to be in touch with the truth and to be able to express it, openly and naturally and without the shallow artifice of commerce."[83]

Soul implied depth of spirit, a connection to what was uniquely hip and black. It was, said writer William L. Van Deburg, "essential to an understanding of the culture of Black Power ... If there was beauty and emotion in blackness, soul made it so ... Soul was sass—a type of primal spiritual energy and passionate joy."[84] However, one was not necessarily born with soul. Only those whose black consciousness had been raised had it. It implied a belief in the movement and a belief in the self.

Sam Cooke's 1965 song "A Change Is Gonna Come" became a significant anthem for the civil rights movement and Black Arts movement.

The Evolution of Black Music

The black arts were never a secret. Baraka and other artists promoted their ideas and ideals loudly and frequently. Yet the intense politics and radical tactics were too militant and too angry for some in the general public. Pop music, on the other hand, was broadly accepted.

Berry Gordy's Motown Records transformed the Motor City of Detroit into Hitsville, U.S.A. Accomplished recording artists such as Diana Ross and the Supremes, Smokey Robinson and the Miracles, and the Temptations put soul music on everyone's radar and radio dials. However, while the earliest Motown releases spoke of innocent love or the loss of it, ideas first voiced by the Black Arts movement began catching on with race-conscious songwriters and performers.

In 1966, black singer Stevie Wonder recorded white folk singer Bob Dylan's "Blowin' in the Wind." This was an example of a popular black artist recording a song that reflected the true tenor of the times. Wonder's 1973 album *Innervisions* included an attack on disgraced president Richard Nixon as well as the long and plaintive "Living for the City," a story-song about a southern black family whose son travels to New York City and is arrested and jailed for a crime he did not commit. Wonder's work would continue to be filled with Black Arts consciousness.

Spoken word poet Gil Scott-Heron confronted politics even more directly in 1970. Aggressively speaking over an African drumbeat, Scott-Heron aimed to rile black Americans enough to get them out into the streets and participate because, he said, "The revolution will not be televised,"[85] in his song of the same name. Scott-Heron's producer, Bob Thiele, recorded mostly jazz musicians, including John Coltrane, but Thiele clearly saw Scott-Heron's power as a politically progressive artist. According to historian Mark Anthony Neal, Scott-Heron and Wonder "had a significant impact ... while functioning in very traditional roles as artists in tune with the social, cultural, and political imagination of the larger African-American community."[86]

The next year, in 1971, Motown star Marvin Gaye was primed to make a statement. After the death of his singing partner, Tammi Terrell, Gaye had considered retiring from the music business until Four Tops singer Renaldo Benson approached Gaye with an idea for a new song—a song about black America's confusing and painful present. Gaye, Benson, and songwriter Al Cleveland's collaboration

Spoken word poet and performer Gil Scott-Heron touched on many social and political issues in his poetry and music.

of the Black Power and Black Arts movements. While some critics at the time may have considered Gaye's message of unity naive, a 2004 issue of *Rolling Stone* magazine voted the song as the fourth-greatest song of all time.

"Black popular music provided a sonic backdrop to the efforts of the new militants who had made a psychic break from the church-based song generally associated with the civil rights movement," Jeffrey O. G. Ogbar wrote. "For black nationalists, the old Negro spirituals were antiquated rituals of a more passive ... struggle."[87] Other politically conscious artists such as funk group War, James Brown, and Edwin Starr also apparently spoke for writers like Baraka, who continued calling for "an art that would reach the people, that would take them higher, ready them for war and victory, as popular as the Impressions or the Miracles or Marvin Gaye."[88]

However, this dream of a more politically driven art never became a complete reality. Popular culture eventually moved away from the radical political tactics of the Black Arts movement.

yielded "What's Going On." The tune begins with the jovial sounds of black men gathering and greeting one another. After a moment, an alto saxophone snakes its way over an echoing drumbeat. While the song is antiwar in its sentiments, Gaye could be speaking about the Vietnam War or the race war raging on America's streets, or both. "What's Going On" makes a stark case for understanding and healing, a far cry from the sometimes-brutal rhetoric

MAYA ANGELOU
AND LUCILLE CLIFTON

Despite their relatively low profile during the Black Arts movement, female writers began lighting a new "black fire" in the mid to late 1970s. Maya Angelou, born in 1928 in Missouri, worked as a dancer, singer, and actor. In the 1950s, she toured Europe as part of the cast of the opera *Porgy and Bess*. In the early 1960s, she met Martin Luther King Jr. and later became close friends with Malcolm X. Her first published work, *I Know Why the Caged Bird Sings*, was released in 1969. This autobiography chronicles the first 17 years of Angelou's life, including her rape by her mother's boyfriend, after which Angelou did not speak for five years. Angelou continued to publish plays and poems, winning a Pulitzer Prize in 1972. On May 28, 2014, Angelou died at her home in Winston-Salem, North Carolina, after suffering from heart failure at the age of 86.

Lucille Clifton was raised modestly in Depew, New York. Neither of her parents had a formal education, but they inspired Clifton to read by buying her books. In her 20s, Clifton developed a minimalist style of poetry, meaning she used few words to express herself. Her brand of free verse often concentrates on the body, as in her most famous poem "Homage to My Hips." The poem reads:

Music would remain an essential tool for continuing the struggle, though, long after the Black Arts movement had officially passed into history. The emergence of new genres in the coming years, such as rap and hip-hop music, would serve as an extension of the ideas born out of the Black Arts movement, and many of these new artists would carry these messages of black empowerment into this new day and age.

African Americans in Film

Another popular art form African Americans had influence on during this time was film. Before the 1970s, black people were rarely portrayed on screen. When they were, white screenwriters placed them in secondary roles, as butlers, maids, and chauffeurs. Black writers were occasionally hired, as Langston Hughes was to write the film *Way Down South* in 1939, but the final results often

these hips are big hips
they need space to
move around in.
they don't fit into little
petty places. these hips
are free hips.
they don't like to be held back.
these hips have never been enslaved,
they go where they want to go
they do what they want to do.
these hips are mighty hips.
these hips are magic hips.
i have known them
to put a spell on a man and
spin him like a top![1]

Maya Angelou is one of the most influential female African American writers.

Like Angelou, Clifton's work is uniquely feminine and strong. Her honors include serving as Maryland's poet laureate and two grants from the National Endowment for the Arts.

1. Quoted in Patrice Vecchione, ed., *The Body Eclectic: An Anthology of Poems.* New York, NY: Henry Holt, 2002, p. 65.

played like watered-down or white versions of the black experience. One exception, Oscar Micheaux's all-black *The Homesteader* in 1919, did not receive wide release. Yet Micheaux dreamed of a day when it would be different: "I'm tired of reading about the Negro in an inferior position in society. I want to see them in dignified roles. Also, I want to see the white man and the white woman as the villains ... I want to see the Negro picture in books just like he lives."[89]

Some strides were made early on. Kansas native Hattie McDaniel won the Best Supporting Actress Academy Award for her role as Mammy in 1939's blockbuster *Gone with the Wind*, making her the first African American to win an Oscar. Paul Robeson, a civil rights activist, singer, and actor, made waves as much for his politics as for his memorable rendition of "Ol' Man River" from the 1936 musical film *Show Boat*.

Hattie McDaniel (right) won the Academy Award for Best Supporting Actress in 1939 for her portrayal of Mammy in Gone With the Wind *alongside Vivien Leigh (left).*

Even more controversial than Robeson, at least in film terms, was Lincoln Perry, who used the stage name Stepin Fetchit. He became a comic performer as a teenager, performing in the popular minstrel shows of the early 20th century. He sometimes performed in blackface makeup, and he was labeled as "the Laziest Man in the World." While this persona offended many African Americans, Fetchit eventually brought his act to the silver screen and became the first black actor to receive featured screen credit in a film. He was also the first black actor to earn a million dollars.

Yet even before the Black Arts movement seeped into the public consciousness in the 1960s, Hollywood studios sought to cash in with people of color without alienating their white audiences. Actors such as the debonair Sidney Poitier and the comic Bill Cosby represented Hollywood's mainstream version of black America—smart, tough, yet acceptable to whites. Despite this cinematic change, the reality for many black Americans, especially those living in America's inner cities, was still not reflected in their local theaters.

While the big studios were grappling with the subject of race on film, independent filmmaker Melvin Van Peebles had his own ideas. In 1970, he released *Watermelon Man*, about a white racist who wakes up in the body of a black man, starring Godfrey Cambridge. While the film's popularity quickly attracted the eyes of Hollywood executives, they shunned his next movie in 1971. However, black audiences did not. Van Peebles is seen today as the father of blaxploitation cinema. The word combines *blax*, a slang version of black, and *ploitation*, an abbreviated version of exploitation. The implication—and often the reality—suggested the use of stereotypes, or broad, insulting portrayals of both African Americans and whites. Yet young and hungry filmmakers were intent on shattering the old image of black people in film on their terms.

Shaft and *Super Fly*

In 1971, noted photographer Gordon Parks agreed to direct *Shaft*, a studio-financed detective drama with a major difference: The cop was black, and so were many of the criminals. Starring Richard Roundtree, the film presented an assertive, flirtatious tough guy detective named John Shaft. Director Parks, though, remained uneasy about the genre his film was placed in. "I never associated *Shaft* with black exploitation ... Why is having a black hero who for the first time stood up for what he believed and fought the system ... why call it an exploitation film?"[90] Historian Donald Bogle agreed, saying that *Shaft* "essentially was a standard white detective tale enlivened by a black sensibility."[91] Notably, the "Theme from *Shaft*" by Isaac Hayes went to the top of the pop charts. Hayes also won the Academy Award for Best Original Song in 1972, making him the first African American to win that honor. There were also two follow-up films released featuring Roundtree, *Shaft's Big Score!* (1972) and *Shaft in Africa* (1973), as well as a *Shaft* TV series from 1973 to 1974.

A remake of *Shaft* was made in 2000 starring Samuel L. Jackson as Shaft. The film grossed over $107 million worldwide and received mixed reviews. Another *Shaft* remake featuring Jackson was released on June 14, 2019.

In 1972, Parks's son, Gordon Jr., directed *Super Fly*. The film's hero was no John Shaft, however. Instead, Priest (played by Ron O'Neal) dealt cocaine and violently battled his enemies. This portrayal of a strong, confident black man making money appealed to the new generation of African American youth, as the generation before them had suffered through the segregation, sit-ins, and marches to try to gain equal rights. However, organizations such as the National Association for the Advancement of Colored People (NAACP) and the Congress of Racial Equality (CORE) joined a coalition attempting to stop the movie's distribution, as they, along with many African Americans, were displeased with the images of "black males as pimps, dope pushers, gangsters, and super males,"[92] shown in the film. Despite their efforts, the film was a huge success, earning $11 million in its first two months of release. Although it traded on black and white stereotypes like so many other such films, Hollywood finally became virtually color blind: The only color it saw now was green. A remake of the film, directed by Director X, titled *SuperFly* was released in 2018.

Over the next 10 years, hundreds of blaxploitation pictures were

Richard Roundtree played the role of detective John Shaft in the 1970s.

KWANZAA AND JUNETEENTH

In the mid-1960s, university professor Maulana Karenga founded Us, a black nationalist group that rivaled the Black Panthers. Karenga led his own demonstrations and developed his own ideas on Black Power. Yet today Karenga is best known as the creator of Kwanzaa, a yearly celebration of African traditions. Taken from the Swahili phrase *matunda ya kwanzaa*, meaning "first fruits of the harvest," Kwanzaa is based on the ancient harvest rituals of Egypt and Nubia. Each year, many African Americans set aside December 26 to January 1 as a time to share with family. Often, traditional African clothes are worn and candles are lit as loved ones gather for a feast consisting of African delicacies. Gifts for children must include a book and a heritage symbol—a commitment to history and tradition.

Since its inception, Kwanzaa's popularity has only grown. Yet unlike other winter holidays such as Christmas and Hanukkah, it is not a religious celebration. Instead, said Karenga, "Kwanzaa brings a cultural message which speaks to the best of what it means to be African and human in the fullest sense."[1]

Another holiday created by African Americans was Juneteenth, which is also known as Juneteenth Independence Day or Freedom Day. It is the celebration commemorating the day of June 19, 1865, when the abolition of slavery was announced in Texas, and also the emancipation of enslaved African Americans throughout the South. Some traditions for this holiday include public readings of the Emancipation Proclamation; singing songs, such as "Swing Low, Sweet Chariot" and "Lift Every Voice and Sing;" and reading the works of famous African American writers such as Maya Angelou and Ralph Ellison.

1. Maulana Karenga, "The Founder's Welcome," The Official Kwanzaa Web Site. www.officialkwanzaawebsite.org.

produced. Titles included *Black Belt Jones*, *Dolemite*, and *Foxy Brown*, starring the attractive, Afro-wearing Pam Grier. Studios pumped films such as these out for high box office returns on their modest production investments.

Black Novelists

During the Black Arts movement, the primary means of artistic expressions were poetry, drama, and music. Yet fiction never completely went away. Novelists such as Hal Bennett and Henry Dumas published important work in the 1960s and 1970s, but the mass appeal of novels did not return until the Black Arts movement was officially over.

Two of the most important writers to emerge after the end of the Black Arts movement were Toni Morrison and Alice Walker. While only a handful of women received wide acclaim during the movement's heyday, Morrison and Walker found wide acceptance and popularity with both black and white audiences.

Morrison, for one, recognized the importance of the Black Arts movement's vision. However, the former book editor never directly involved herself. "I think all good art has always been political ... Art becomes [a] mere soap-box not because it's too political but because the artist isn't any good at what he's doing."[93] She forged a unique and powerful body of work. Her novels *Sula*, *The Bluest Eye*, and *Beloved* are considered modern classics. In 1993, Morrison became the first black woman to be awarded the Nobel Prize in Literature, considered the highest award any writer can receive. Playwright Wole Soyinka was the first black person to receive this award in 1986.

Walker also found mainstream literary success in the years following the demise of the Black Arts movement.

Her best-known novel, 1982's *The Color Purple*, centers on a poor, abused woman named Celie who, after being raped by her stepfather, is married off to a brutal man, referred to only as Mister. For years after, Celie writes to God about her pain. She is most heartbroken by her separation from her dear sister, Nettie, who has found a new life in Africa. In 1983, *The Color Purple* won Walker the Pulitzer Prize for Fiction and the National Book Award for Fiction. Yet Walker, unlike Morrison, almost completely distanced herself from the legacy of the Black Arts movement, said biographer Evelyn C. White: "Having written a novel in which the theme of black accountability superceded the racism of whites ... Alice was clearly not in step with Black Arts ideology."[94]

In spite of Walker's rejection, a host of black artists did embrace the basic tenets of the Black Arts and Black Power movements. As the 20th century drew to a close, legions of young musicians, poets, novelists, and dramatists heard the call. They embraced the best—and sometimes the worst—aspects of the Black Arts movement, forging new messages for a new generation and pushing "blackness" and black voices into the mainstream of American life.

Toni Morrison was the first black woman to win the Nobel Prize in Literature in 1993.

As Black Power lost its grip on the nation in 1975, artists of color continued creating but did so without an official movement behind them. Then again, Black Arts had always been less a single entity than a collection of artists and intellectuals working toward the common goals of unity, liberation, and self-reliance. Black Arts promoted the recognition that "the souls of black folk were valuable, worthy, even sacred,"[95] William L. Van Deburg wrote. By fusing the artist and the community, a unique and transformative bond was formed.

Baraka Controversy

For one of the movement's leaders, the fading of Black Arts served only as an important step on a lifelong journey. In 1974, Baraka renounced black nationalism in favor of Marxism. From that time on, Baraka focused his attention more globally on native African peoples and their struggle for liberation. For some in the Black Arts movement, this shift was a betrayal of the cause. However, according to author Jerry Gafio Watts, "Baraka claimed to have intensified his commitment to the emancipation of black America, arguing that Marxism was the logical next step for any sound thinking, revolutionary, black nationalist."[96]

In 2001, Baraka stirred up some controversy while serving a term as New Jersey's poet laureate. He wrote the poem "Somebody Blew Up America," which was a response to the September 11 terrorist attacks that left more than 3,000 people dead. The poem contained a passage that has since become infamous in which Baraka asked who knew of the imminent attacks. His strong suspicion, the poem implies, is that the Israeli government did. Israel has long been an ally of the United States. The poem "was not only anti-Semitic, but it was also insulting to members of families who had to suffer the death of relatives on 9/11,"[97] said Shai Goldstein, the regional director of the Anti-Defamation League. Coming to his own defense, Baraka said, "Everything said about Israel in the poem is easily researched ... If you criticize Israel, they hide behind the religion and call you anti-Semitic."[98] The governor of New Jersey, Jim McGreevey, asked Baraka to resign from his post as state poet laureate; however, Baraka refused. Although McGreevey could not legally remove Baraka from his post, in 2003, he convinced New Jersey legislators to abolish the honor in its entirety.

Baraka's outspokenness was only one part of the Black Power and Black Arts legacy. It is a legacy that extends beyond traditional poetry, music, and drama. "Black Power quickly came to mean very different things to different people," historian Manning Marable wrote. "For the black entrepreneurs who manipulated blackness to sell goods and services in poor urban communities, Black Power was a demand to control black consumer markets."[99]

Politically Conscious Rap and Hip-Hop

As the influence of black arts dimmed, consumerism, typically in the form of rap and hip-hop music, rose up to take its place, giving birth to the hip-hop movement of the mid-1970s. Poor residents in black communities created this influential cultural movement in the South Bronx section of New York City. Hip-hop later became a billion-dollar industry with a worldwide reach. The genre has influenced the way people make music, the way they dance, and the way they wear their clothes. It has also shaped people's political views and turned many people into entrepreneurs.

Throughout the late 1970s and early 1980s, rappers such as Kurtis Blow, Run DMC, and Sugarhill Gang produced albums that spoke of inner-city black life with a sense of street credibility that black (and white) youth responded to. The 1983 rap record "White Lines (Don't Do It)" by Melle Mel encouraged young people to avoid the temptations of cocaine, addiction, and selling drugs with memorable lines and a danceable beat. Although such records would in time give way to heavier and more violent gangsta rap, many artists carried on the Black Arts' tradition of revolution.

Public Enemy was a hip-hop group founded by Chuck D (front right) and Flavor Flav (front left). Terminator X (center) was brought in as the group's first DJ. He was later replaced by DJ Lord in 1999.

Perhaps the most influential hip-hop group of the late 1980s and early 1990s was Public Enemy, led by Chuck D and Flavor Flav. Their unique brand of politically conscious rap and their devotion to black communities had long been popular with inner-city African Americans. Albums such as their debut *Yo! Bum Rush the Show* in 1987 and *It Takes a Nation of Millions to Hold Us Back* a year later owed much in the way of articulation and attitude to the Black Arts movement.

While the hip-hop movement proved to be lucrative for those who were involved, it did not completely help to solve the issues with race in America. The movement was one that tried to unite people from all backgrounds through music and art. However, as time passed, new challenges would arise, reminding the country that to form a nation of equality among all races, it has to examine its weaknesses and try to build a stronger foundation for all its people.

CHAPTER SIX

STRIVING FOR PEACE, EQUALITY, AND UNDERSTANDING

On the evening of February 26, 2012, 17-year-old Trayvon Martin went to a nearby 7-Eleven in Sanford, Florida, and purchased a bag of Skittles and an AriZona beverage. He and his father, Tracy Martin, were visiting and staying with his father's fiancée, who lived in a townhome in a gated community. As he walked back to the gated community, he made a phone call to a girl who was reported to be his girlfriend; however, the call was disconnected. George Zimmerman, a 28-year-old resident and neighborhood watch captain, spotted Martin while sitting in his SUV and called the Sanford Police Department alerting them of "a suspicious person."[100] The police instructed him to stay in his vehicle, which he disregarded. Moments later, a gunshot was heard. Zimmerman claimed he shot the black teen in self-defense, but millions of other people disagreed and instead claimed that he intentionally murdered Martin. In February 2015, Zimmerman was acquitted of all charges, as there was not enough evidence for a federal hate crime prosecution.

Since this incident, there have been numerous high-profile altercations involving unarmed African Americans being killed by police, such as Eric Garner in New York City and Freddie Gray in Baltimore, Maryland, and also much younger black teens, such as 18-year-old Michael Brown Jr. from Ferguson, Missouri, and 12-year-old Tamir Rice from Cleveland, Ohio.

After Martin was fatally shot, the Black Lives Matter organization was created. They aim to expose incidences of police brutality, protest against racism, and liberate those who have been marginalized by the color of their skin. Out of all race demographics in the United States, black people are most likely to be killed by police. They are also three times more likely to be killed by police than white people.

Another shocking incident, which was labeled as a hate crime, was the mass shooting at the Emanuel African Methodist Episcopal Church in Charleston, South Carolina, referred to as the Charleston church shooting, or massacre. Dylann Roof, a 21-year-old white supremacist, murdered nine African Americans during a prayer service at the church on the evening of June 17, 2015. The morning after the shooting, when Roof was arrested by police, he admitted to the shooting and said he had hoped he would ignite a race war.

In response to the massacre, President Barack Obama expressed his sadness and anger in a televised statement: "This type of mass violence does not happen in other advanced countries. It doesn't happen in other places with this kind of frequency. And it is within our power to do something about it."[101] The NAACP also offered up a statement: "The NAACP was founded to fight against racial hatred and we are outraged that 106 years later, we are faced today with another mass hate crime ... There is no greater

People protested outside the Seminole County Courthouse in Sanford, Florida, demanding the arrest of George Zimmerman.

coward than a criminal who enters a house of God and slaughters innocent people engaged in the study of scripture."[102] In December 2016, Roof was convicted of 33 federal hate crime and murder charges. He was sentenced to death on January 10, 2017.

Black Activism Through Modern Television and Film

As many tragic events within black communities in the United States occur, artists continue to carry on the tradition of activism through art that was started by the Black Arts movement. Several of today's films and television shows present real and complex stories of African American experiences, helping eradicate stereotypes facing the black community. Many of these works showcase characters having to face racial struggles in America and how they overcome these obstacles.

The 2016 film *Moonlight*, featuring actor Trevante Rhodes as Chiron, presents three stages of his life—as a young boy, a teenager, and a young adult—and follows him as he explores his identity and sexuality and reflects on the physical and emotional abuse he endured growing up. The film also takes a look at black masculinity, an aspect of African American culture that tends to fall under harsh and critical stereotypes

since many expect black males to always be strong and overly masculine. The film, based on Tarell Alvin McCraney's play *In Moonlight Black Boys Look Blue*, closely based on his own life experiences, received high praise, as Justin Chang of the *Los Angeles Times* wrote, "[Director Barry Jenkins] made a film that urges the viewer to look past Chiron's outward appearance and his superficial signifiers of identity, climbing inside familiar stereotypes in order to quietly dismantle them from within ... [*Moonlight*] doesn't say much; it says everything."[103] In addition to glowing reviews, the film was nominated for eight Oscars and won three—Best Picture, Best Supporting Actor, and Best Adapted Screenplay—at the 89th Academy Awards in 2017.

Another film that came out the same year as *Moonlight* was *Hidden Figures*, which told the true story of three African American women—Katherine Johnson (played by Taraji P. Henson), Dorothy Vaughan (played by Octavia Spencer), and Mary Jackson (played by Janelle Monáe)—at NASA, who were the brains behind the space launch of John Glenn, the first American astronaut to orbit the Earth. The film is loosely based on the nonfiction book of the same name written by Margot Lee Shetterly about black female mathematicians who worked at NASA during the Space

Race. This film was special because it broke the stereotype that women, and in this particular case black women, are not as capable or qualified to work in STEM (science, technology, engineering, and mathematics) career positions. The film received mostly positive reviews, as one critic wrote, "Hidden Figures is a faithful and truly beautiful portrait of our country's consistent gloss over the racial tensions that have divided and continue to plague the fabric of our existence."[104] At the 89th Academy Awards, the film received three nominations: for Best Adapted Screenplay, Best Picture, and Best Supporting Actress.

The TV show *black-ish,* featuring an upper middle class African-American family, began airing on ABC in 2014. The show has brought up themes surrounding racism, police brutality, LGBT+ rights, and more. In the 40th episode, titled "Hope," the family witnesses news reports of an unarmed black man's run-in with the police. While the case they are witnessing is fictional, it is reminiscent of many recent events involving unarmed black people and the police. The family has a back-and-forth discussion about the situation, addressing both sides of the

The 2016 film Moonlight *won three Oscars at the 89th Academy Awards in 2017.*

issue of police brutality and not completely vilifying the police force. This show has been recognized as a piece of media that discusses current events involving relevant and engaging cultural topics and has received praise from many critics. The show has received Emmy and Golden Globe nominations over the years, with Tracee Ellis Ross winning the Golden Globe Award for Best Actress in a Television Series Musical or Comedy in 2017.

Black Music of Today

While the themes within rap and hip-hop became violent with gangsta rap in the mid-1980s and early 1990s, several artists maintained the politically conscious aspect of the previous versions of this music. Some would argue that even gangsta rap embodied the same revolutionary mindset that the Black Arts and Black Power movements did. Today, there are many rap and hip-hop artists who create politically conscious music, such as Kendrick Lamar, Lupe Fiasco, and Childish Gambino.

Lamar has made commentary on the racism and stereotypes black people in America face in his music. His 2015 album *To Pimp a Butterfly* and 2017 album *DAMN.* both brought up several

aspects of the black experience, such as police brutality, and presented it to a wide audience. Arcade Fire's Will Butler labeled Lamar's 2015 album "a pantheon for racial empowerment" and acknowledged it as a conscious hip-hop record that "will be revered not just at the top of some list at the end of the year, but in the

Kendrick Lamar's commentary on racial inequality, police brutality, and gun control in his music has sparked controversy and has gotten people talking about these important issues.

subconscious of music fans for decades to come."[105] Matthew Trammell described Lamar's *DAMN.* as "a wide-screen masterpiece of rap, full of expensive beats, furious rhymes, and peerless storytelling about Kendrick's destiny in America."[106] In April 2018, Lamar was awarded with a Pulitzer Prize in music for *DAMN.* In the 75-year history of the award, it is the first time a popular artist and a hip-hop artist received the award.

Rap and hip-hop are not the only popular musical genres presenting these ideas about racism and African American life. R&B artists, such as Janelle Monáe and Solange have also made significant contributions in music that have made society think about the current state of race in America and the world. Monáe's 2018 album *Dirty Computer* received rave reviews from music critics, one of which said, "Dirty Computer sounds like 2018 distilled into a sci-fi funk pop extravaganza by a female Black Panther."[107] Themes explored on this album include Black Power, racism, sexism, sexuality, and more.

Solange is another artist who has delved into discussing what it is like to be a young black person in today's America. Her 2016 album *A Seat at the Table* touches on themes of prejudice, blackness, relationships, and identity. Her song "Don't Touch My Hair" is a standout track, which highlights the uncomfortable experience many African Americans go through when people ask to touch their hair. These

Janelle Monáe's album Dirty Computer *speaks to the current state of racial inequality in America.*

people do not realize this is seen as objectifying and is, in fact, an invasion of personal space.

In March 2019, Solange released her album *When I Get Home*, which is about her reminiscing and exploring her childhood hometown of Houston, Texas. She looks back at her history and considers what her future as a black woman in this world will be. It can also be seen as a celebration of black womanhood and feminism. Throughout the album, there are lines of poetry read during interludes, such as a poem by Pat Parker, an African-American lesbian and feminist poet and activist, and Phylicia Rashad and Debbie Allen reading snippets of their mother Vivian Ayers's poem "On Status." A reviewer described the album, writing that it "give[s] voice to the endless frustration of being black in the world, to be punished on that basis, and to support the urge we all often feel to push back against it all."[108]

Carrying on the Legacy of the Black Arts Movement

American popular culture is now comprised of more images of African Americans than ever before. Each segment of art has welcomed more people of color and continues to push for their visibility and appreciation as artists.

One of Jordan Peele's main priorities as a director is to cast black actors as the main characters in his films. The African American director, who has released two successful horror films, *Get Out* in 2017 and *Us* in 2019, features black leading characters. In an interview with the *Hollywood Reporter*, he said:

> *The way I look at it, I get to cast black people in my movies. I feel fortunate to be in this position where I can say to Universal, 'I want to make a $20 million horror movie with a black family.' And they say yes ... I don't see myself casting a white dude as the lead in my movie. Not that I don't like white dudes ... But I've seen that movie.*[109]

After hearing this comment from Peele, some of his critics claimed he was being racist by excluding white male leads from his movies. However, he was only stating how he believes his purpose as a director is to give "a voice and opportunities to those traditionally underrepresented in front and behind the camera, be it gender, race or sexual orientation."[110]

Black poets, novelists, musical artists, actors, and artists of all kinds continue to flourish today. "Today's black

Jordan Peele won his first Academy Award in 2018 for Best Original Screenplay for his film Get Out.

arts scene," Henry Louis Gates Jr. wrote, "is characterized by an awareness of previous black traditions, which these [new] artists echo, imitate, parody, and revise, self-consciously, in acts of 'riffing' or 'signifying' or even 'sampling.'"[111]

Such sampling is an homage to past artists and a look forward as novelists, musicians, dancers, and painters build new monuments to the complexity and beauty of human experience. However, unlike the work of the Black Arts movement, these new creations invite all people, regardless of color, to look and listen. The politics are still there, the struggle for equality and understanding continues, yet "today's African-American artists increasingly strike themes that are racially and culturally universal,"[112] Jack E. White wrote.

The Future of Black Arts

Like most legends, the birth of the Black Arts movement following the death of Malcolm X contains seeds of truth and a host of misconceptions. Yet one thing is certain: The Black Arts movement continues influencing contemporary American culture. Echoes of it reside in the socially conscious hip-hop/funk of artists like the Roots, whose early album title *Things Fall Apart* is taken from Nigerian writer Chinua Achebe's novel of the same name, as well as the novels and stories of Edward P. Jones, Pulitzer Prize–winning author of *The Known World*.

"The mission," Madhubuti wrote, "is how do we become a whole people, and how do we begin to essentially tell our narrative, while at the same time move toward a level of success in this country and in the world?"[113] Madhubuti does not suggest a complete answer. Yet what is clear is that today more people of all ethnicities want to listen to, share in, sympathize with, and understand the African American experience. The true legacy of the Black Arts movement is still evolving, but before long, the revolution that the Black Arts movement began may become unnecessary. "If the mission of these black artists succeeds," wrote Gates, "the very need to declare a 'renaissance' ... may be unnecessary, which means that today's may truly be the renaissance to end all renaissances."[114]

As long as there is racism, there will always be people speaking up for minorities through art as a means to communicate that equality is deserved by all. Activists and black artists today are using their voices and art to speak up for those minorities, bringing these issues to light and to the forefront of society. If these issues continue to arise and the divide in the United States continues to widen, hopefully artists can help Americans understand each other better, make them realize what all people deserve, and show people that they should all treat each other with kindness and respect.

NOTES

Introduction: Early History of Black Art

1. Quoted in Alex Haley, *The Autobiography of Malcolm X*. New York, NY: Ballantine, 1973, p. 175.

2. Quoted in David Farber and Beth Bailey, *The Columbia Guide to America in the 1960s*. New York, NY: Columbia University Press, 2001, p. 61.

3. James Edward Smethurst, *The Black Arts Movement: Literary Nationalism in the 1960s and 1970s*. Chapel Hill, NC: University of North Carolina Press, 2005, p. 25.

4. Henry Louis Gates Jr., "Black Creativity: On the Cutting Edge," *TIME*, October 10, 1994. content.time.com/time/magazine/article/0,9171,981564,00.html.

5. Gates, "Black Creativity."

Chapter One: The Origins of Black Nationalism

6. Quoted in Adam Hochschild, *Bury the Chains: Prophets and Rebels in the Fight to Free an Empire's Slaves*. Boston, MA: Mariner, 2006, p. 32.

7. Charles George, *Life Under the Jim Crow Laws*. San Diego, CA: Lucent Press, 2000, p. 10.

8. Anupuw Ptah, "Look For Me In The Whirlwind ~ The Marcus Garvey Story," YouTube video, 2:14:08, December 29, 2016. www.youtube.com/watch?v=LsypjWJ7MpU.

9. Quoted in Robert A. Hill, ed., *The Marcus Garvey and Universal Negro Improvement Association Papers, Vol. 1, 1826-August 1919*. Berkeley, CA: University of California Press, 1983, p. 5.

10. Ptah, "Look For Me In The Whirlwind."

11. Ptah, "Look For Me In The Whirlwind."

12. Ptah, "Look For Me In The Whirlwind."

13. Quoted in Robert J. Norrell, *The House I Live In: Race in the American Century*. Oxford, England: Oxford University Press, 2005, p. 96.

14. Robert J. Norrell, *The House I Live In*, p. 97.

15. Langston Hughes, "The Negro Artist and the Racial Mountain," *Nation,* last updated March 11, 2002. www.thenation.com/article/negro-artist-and-racial-mountain/.

16. Hughes, "The Negro Artist and the Racial Mountain."

17. Ralph Ellison, *Invisible Man*. New York, NY: Vintage, 1981, p. 3.

18. Quoted in Farber and Bailey, *The Columbia Guide to America in the 1960s*, p. 48.

Chapter Two: The Emergence of the Black Arts Movement

19. Quoted in Haley, *The Autobiography of Malcolm X*, p. 440.

20. Quoted in Haley, *The Autobiography of Malcolm X*, p. 442.

21. Quoted in Haley, *The Autobiography of Malcolm X*, p. 442.

22. Quoted in Haley, *The Autobiography of Malcolm X*, p. 442.

23. Amiri Baraka, *The Autobiography of LeRoi Jones*. Chicago, IL: Lawrence Hill Books, 1997, p. 296.

24. Baraka, *The Autobiography of LeRoi Jones*, p. 285.

25. Baraka, *The Autobiography of LeRoi Jones*, p. 295.

26. Quoted in Peniel E. Joseph, *Waiting 'til the Midnight Hour: A Narrative History of Black Power in America*. New York, NY: Holt, 2006, p. 256.

27. Baraka, *The Autobiography of LeRoi Jones*, p. 307.

28. Smethurst, *The Black Arts Movement*, p. 103.

29. Smethurst, *The Black Arts Movement*, p. 106.

30. Quoted in Floyd W. Hayes III et al., eds., *A Turbulent Voyage: Readings in African American Studies*. Lanham, MD: Rowman and Littlefield, 2000, p. 237.

31. George Breitman, "In Defense of Black Power," *International Socialist Review*, vol. 28, no. 1, January-February 1967.

32. Quoted in Valerie Reitman and Mitchell Landsberg, "Watts Riots, 40 Years Later," *Los Angeles Times*, August 11, 2005. articles.latimes.com/2005/aug/11/local/la-me-watts11aug11.

33. Quoted in Reitman and Landsberg, "Watts Riots, 40 Years Later."

Chapter Three: Groundbreaking Cultural Influencers

34. Manning Marable, *Living Black History: How Reimagining the African-American Past Can Remake America's Racial Future*. New York, NY: Basic Civitas, 2006, p. 96.

35. Quoted in Ebere Onwudiwe and Minabere Ibelema, eds., *Afro-Optimism: Perspectives on Africa's Advances*. Westport, CT: Praeger, 2003, pp. 55–56.

36. Quoted in Michael L. Krenn, *Fall-Out Shelters for the Human Spirit: American Art and the Cold War.* Chapel Hill, NC: University of North Carolina Press, 2005, p. 187.

37. Larry Neal, "The Black Writer's Role," *Liberator*, June 1966, p. 8.

38. Quoted in Frantz Fanon, *The Wretched of the Earth.* New York, NY: Grove, 1968, cover.

39. Fanon, *The Wretched of the Earth*, p. 39.

40. Fanon, *The Wretched of the Earth*, p. 94.

41. LeRoi Jones, *Blues People: Negro Music in White America.* New York, NY: William Morrow, 1999, p. ix.

42. Geoffrey C. Ward, *Jazz: A History of America's Music.* New York, NY: Knopf, 2000, p. 413.

43. Quoted in Ward, *Jazz*, p. 413.

44. Quoted in Ward, *Jazz*, p. 434.

45. Quoted in Ward, *Jazz*, p. 436.

46. Quoted in Faye Anderson, "John Coltrane and Civil Rights," All That Philly Jazz, June 19, 2017. phillyjazz.us/2017/06/19/john-coltrane-and-civil-rights/.

47. Quoted in Howard Dodson, *Jubilee: The Emergence of African-American Culture.* Washington, DC: National Geographic Books, 2002, p. 186.

48. Nina Simone and Stephen Cleary, *I Put a Spell on You: The Autobiography of Nina Simone.* New York, NY: Da Capo, 2003, p. 89.

49. Joseph, *Waiting 'til the Midnight Hour*, p. 55.

50. Joseph, *Waiting 'til the Midnight Hour*, p. 56.

51. Quoted in Joseph, *Waiting 'til the Midnight Hour*, p. 55.

52. Quoted in Joseph, *Waiting 'til the Midnight Hour*, p. 90.

53. Quoted in Joseph, *Waiting 'til the Midnight Hour*, p. 90.

54. Quoted in Barbara Maranzani, "Martin Luther King Jr. and Malcolm X Only Met Once," Biography, February 12, 2019. www.biography.com/news/martin-luther-king-jr-malcolm-x-meeting.

55. Quoted in Maranzani, "Martin Luther King Jr. and Malcolm X Only Met Once."

Chapter Four: To Conform or Not to Conform?

56. Quoted in Hayes, *A Turbulent Voyage*, p. 236.

57. Jerry Gafio Watts, *Amiri Baraka: The Politics and Art of a Black Intellectual.* New York, NY: New York University Press, 2001, p. 201.

58. Quoted in Watts, *Amiri Baraka*, p. 201.

59. Quoted in Watts, *Amiri Baraka*, p. 201.

60 Quoted in Fritz Gysin and Christopher Mulvey, eds., *Black Liberation in the Americas.* Münster, Germany: LIT Verlag, 2001, p. 203.

61. Quoted in Robert A. Pratt, *Selma's Bloody Sunday: Protest, Voting Rights, and the Struggle for Racial Equality.* Baltimore, MD: John Hopkins University Press, 2017, p. 114.

62. Quoted in stellastey, "63 Black Power Salute," YouTube video, 3:28, April 6, 2014. www.youtube.com/watch?v=QCNkW2kNcjw.

63. Quoted in "1968: Black Athletes Make Silent Protest," BBC On This Day, accessed on June 17, 2019. news.bbc.co.uk/onthisday/hi/dates/stories/october/17/newsid_3535000/3535348.stm.

64. Quoted in "1968: Black Athletes Make Silent Protest," BBC On This Day.

65. Quoted in Steve Wyche, "Colin Kaepernick Explains Why He Sat During National Anthem," NFL, August 27, 2016. www.nfl.com/news/story/0ap3000000691077/article/colin-kaepernick-explains-protest-of-national-anthem.

66. Quoted in Mychal Denzel Smith, "Colin Kaepernick's Protest Might Be Unpatriotic. And That's Just Fine," *Guardian*, September 12, 2018. www.theguardian.com/commentisfree/2018/sep/12/colin-kaepernicks-protest-unpatriotic-justice.

67. Quoted in William S. Clayson, *Freedom is Not Enough: The War on Poverty and the Civil Rights Movement in Texas.* Austin, TX: University of Texas Press, 2010, p. 124.

68. Quoted in Henry Hampton and Steve Fayer, *Voices of Freedom: An Oral History of the Civil Rights Movement from the 1950s through the 1980s.* New York, NY: Bantam Books, 1990, p. 523.

69. Quoted in Harry J. Elam Jr. and David Krasner, eds., *African American Performance and Theater History: A Critical Reader.* New York, NY: Oxford University Press, 2000, p. 56.

70. Quoted in Elam and Krasner, *African American Performance and Theater History*, pp. 56–57.

71. Quoted in "Interview with William O'Neal," Washington University Digital Library, April 13, 1989. digital.wustl.edu/e/eii/eiiweb/one5427.1047.125williamo'neal.html.

72. Robert J. Norrell, *The House I Live In: Race in the American Century*. New York, NY: Oxford University Press, 2005, pp. 262–263.

73. Quoted in Hampton and Fayer, *Voices of Freedom*, p. 358.

74. Joseph, *Waiting 'til the Midnight Hour*, p. 214.

75. Joseph, *Waiting 'til the Midnight Hour*, p. 215.

76. Joseph, *Waiting 'til the Midnight Hour*, p. 216.

77. Henry Louis Gates Jr., *Thirteen Ways of Looking at a Black Man*. New York, NY: Vintage Books, 1997, p. 24.

78. Baraka, *The Autobiography of LeRoi Jones*, p. 311.

Chapter Five: The Movement Goes Mainstream

79. Quoted in "Eyes on the Prize: Ain't Gonna Shuffle No More (1964–1968)," PBS, August 23, 2006. www.shoppbs.pbs.org/wgbh/amex/eyesontheprize/about/pt_205.html.

80. Quoted in "Eyes on the Prize," PBS.

81. Quoted in "Eyes on the Prize," PBS.

82. Quoted in "Eyes on the Prize," PBS.

83. Quoted in Dodson, *Jubilee*, p. 187.

84. William L. Van Deburg, *Black Camelot: African-American Culture Heroes in Their Times, 1960–1980*. Chicago, IL: University of Chicago Press, 1997, p. 73.

85. Gil Scott-Heron, "The Revolution Will Not Be Televised," *Pieces of a Man*, RCA Records, 1971.

86. Mark Anthony Neal, *What the Music Said: Black Popular Music and Black Public Culture*. New York, NY: Routledge, 1999, p. 107.

87. Jeffrey O. G. Ogbar, *Black Power: Radical Politics and African American Identity*. Baltimore, MD: Johns Hopkins University Press, 2005, p. 111.

88. Amiri Baraka, *The LeRoi Jones/Amiri Baraka Reader*. New York, NY: Basic Books, 1991, p. 369.

89. Quoted in Rachel E. Rosenfeld, "Oscar Micheaux's Cinematic Legacy: Through the Eyes of Contemporary Black Newspapers," College of William and Mary, April 26, 2017, p. 102. scholarworks.wm.edu/cgi/viewcontent.cgi?referer=https://www.google.com/&httpsredir=1&article=2093&context=honorstheses.

90. Quoted in S. Torriano Berry and Venise T. Berry, *The 50 Most Influential Black Films: A Celebration of African-American Talent, Determination, and Creativity*. New York, NY: Citadel Press, 2001, p. 123.

91. Donald Bogle, *Toms, Coons, Mulattoes, Mammies, and Bucks: An Interpretive History of Blacks in American Films*. New York, NY: Bloomsbury Publishing, 2016, p. 216.

92. Quoted in Junius Griffin, "Hollywood and the Black Community," *Crisis*, May 1973.

93. Quoted in Danille Taylor-Guthrie, ed., *Conversations with Toni Morrison*. Jackson, MS: University Press of Mississippi, 1994, p. 3.

94. Evelyn C. White, *Alice Walker: A Life*. New York, NY: W. W. Norton, 2004, p. 196.

95. William L. Van Deburg, *New Day in Babylon: The Black Power Movement and American Culture*. Chicago, IL: University of Chicago Press, 1992, p. 186.

96. Watts, *Amiri Baraka*, p. 423.

97. Quoted in Matthew Purdy, "New Jersey Laureate Refuses to Resign Over Poem," *New York Times*, September 28, 2002. www.nytimes.com/2002/09/28/nyregion/new-jersey-laureate-refuses-to-resign-over-poem.html.

98. Quoted in Purdy, "New Jersey Laureate Refuses to Resign Over Poem."

99. Manning Marable, *Speaking Truth to Power: Essays on Race, Resistance, and Racialism*. New York, NY: Perseus, 1998, p. 7.

Chapter Six: Striving for Peace, Equality, and Understanding

100. Quoted in "Trayvon Martin Shooting Fast Facts," CNN, last updated February 28, 2019. www.cnn.com/2013/06/05/us/trayvon-martin-shooting-fast-facts/index.html.

101. Quoted in Larisa Epatko, "Everything We Know About the Charleston Church Shooting," PBS News Hour, June 18, 2015. www.pbs.org/newshour/nation/police-release-photo-suspect-charleston-church-shooting.

102. Quoted in Epatko, "Everything We Know About the Charleston Church Shooting."

103. Justin Chang, "Barry Jenkins' 'Moonlight' Makes the Case For Quiet Eloquence at the Toronto International Film Festival," *Los Angeles Times*, September 11, 2016. www.latimes.com/entertainment/movies/la-et-mn-toronto-2016-barry-jenkins-moonlight-makes-the-case-for-quiet-eloquence-20160911-snap-story.html.

104. Clayton Davis, "Film Review: 'Hidden Figures' is Pure Goodness Featuring a Stellar Cast," awardscircuit.com, December 11, 2016. www.awardscircuit.com/2016/12/11/film-review-hidden-figures-is-pure-goodness-featuring-a-stellar-cast/.

105. Will Butler, "Six Months of Kendrick Lamar's Masterpiece, To Pimp a Butterfly," Gigwise, September 15, 2015. www.gigwise.com/reviews/102811/kendrick-lamar-to-pimp-a-butterfly-6-months-later-feature.

106. Matthew Trammell, "Kendrick Lamar, DAMN.," Pitchfork, April 18, 2017. pitchfork.com/reviews/albums/23147-damn/.

107. Neil McCormick, "It Sounds Like 2018 Distilled Into a Sci-Fi Funk Pop Extravaganza – Janelle Monáe, Dirty Computer, Review," *Telegraph*, April 27, 2018. www.telegraph.co.uk/music/what-to-listen-to/sounds-like-2018-distilled-sci-fi-funk-pop-extravaganza-janelle/.

108. Kuba Shand-Baptiste, "Solange, When I Get Home, Review: An Uplifting Antidote to the Painful Reality Black People Face," *Independent*, March 1, 2019. www.independent.co.uk/arts-entertainment/music/reviews/solange-when-i-get-home-review-tracklist-black-america-trump-poetry-a8803366.html.

109. Quoted in Chris Gardner, "Jordan Peele on Making Movies After 'Us': 'I Don't See Myself Casting a White Dude as the Lead,'" *Hollywood Reporter*, March 26, 2019. www.hollywoodreporter.com/rambling-reporter/jordan-peele-says-i-dont-see-myself-casting-a-white-dude-as-lead-us-1197021.

110. Quoted in Christopher Campbell, "Jordan Peele Signs First-Look Deal With Universal, Begins Bigger-Budget 'Get Out' Follow-Up," Fandango, May 4, 2017. www.fandango.com/movie-news/jordan-peele-signs-first-look-deal-with-universal-begins-bigger-budget-get-out-follow-up-752244.

111. Gates, "Black Creativity."

112. Jack E. White, "The Beauty of Black Art," *TIME*, June 24, 2001. content.time.com/time/magazine/article/0,9171,163036,00.html.

113. Quoted in "An Introduction to the Black Arts Movement," Poetry Foundation, accessed on June 20, 2019. www.poetryfoundation.org/collections/148936/an-introduction-to-the-black-arts-movement.

114. Gates, "Black Creativity."

FOR MORE INFORMATION

Books

Baraka, Amiri. *S O S: Poems 1961-2013*. New York, NY: Grove Press, 2016.
This is a collection of Amiri Baraka's most revolutionary poems that range from his first poems ever published to unpublished pieces he wrote in his final years.

Bracey, John H., Jr., Sonia Sanchez, and James Smethurst. *SOS—Calling All Black People: A Black Arts Movement Reader*. Amherst, MA: University of Massachusetts Press, 2014.
This book displays a collection of writings from the Black Arts movements from iconic writers, such as Amiri Baraka, Nikki Giovanni, Haki Madhubuti, and Sonia Sanchez. In addition to works of fiction, poetry, and drama, it includes critical writings on issues of politics, aesthetics, and gender.

Crawford, Margo Natalie. *Black Post-Blackness: The Black Arts Movement and Twenty-First-Century Aesthetics*. Urbana, IL: University of Illinois Press, 2017.
Crawford makes comparisons between the Black Arts movement and black culture in the 21st century.

Forsgren, La Donna L. *In Search of Our Warrior Mothers: Women Dramatists of the Black Arts Movement*. Evanston, IL: Northwestern University Press, 2018.
This text examines the works and perspectives of four inspirational African American female playwrights from the Black Arts movement.

Mitchell, Verner D., and Cynthia Davis. *Encyclopedia of the Black Arts Movement*. Lanham, MD: Rowman & Littlefield, 2019.
This is a collection of essays from some of the most influential people from the Black Arts movement, such as Maya Angelou, Larry Neal, Amiri Baraka, James Baldwin, Sun Ra, and more.

Websites

African American Museum in Philadelphia

www.aampmuseum.org/
This website provides information about the African American Museum in Philadelphia, known as the first of its kind in the United States. The museum includes four galleries of exhibitions and artifacts, along with frequent dance and music performances. The history of African Americans is charted from the slave trade through the present day.

Amiri Baraka

www.amiribaraka.com
Amiri Baraka's official website includes information about his poems, books, speeches, and essays. There are also sound clips of his poems and a gallery of photographs.

Malcolm X

www.malcolmx.com/
This website dedicated to Malcolm X features a biography, a timeline of noteworthy events in his life, a section detailing his achievements, memorable quotes, and a photo gallery.

National Civil Rights Museum

www.civilrightsmuseum.org
This website features information on the National Civil Rights Museum in Memphis, Tennessee, which was built from the old Lorraine Motel. The museum houses a variety of exhibits, many of which you can touch and experience up close.

Third World Press

thirdworldpressfoundation.org/
The website for Third World Press includes information on the largest independent black-owned publishing house in the United States, and also one of the oldest. Still run from offices in Chicago by Black Arts pioneer Haki Madhubuti, Third World publishes the work of many authors of color, including spoken word poet Gil Scott-Heron and commentator Tavis Smiley.

Zora Neale Hurston

www.zoranealehurston.com/
Zora Neale Hurston's official website includes a biography, news, a list of her books with descriptions, teacher resources, and information about the Zora Neale Hurston Trust, which is represented by The Joy Harris Literary Agency.

INDEX

PICTURE CREDITS

ABOUT THE AUTHOR

Vanessa Oswald is an experienced freelance writer and editor who has written pieces for publications based in New York City and the Western New York area, which include *Resource* magazine, the *Public*, *Auxiliary* magazine, and *Niagara Gazette*. In her spare time, she enjoys dancing, traveling, reading, snowboarding, and attending live concerts.